The Holocaust

Peter Neville

Senior Lecturer in
Twentieth-century European History
The University of Wolverhampton

CAMBRIDGE
UNIVERSITY PRESS

For my former students at Tower Hamlets College

PUBLISHED BY THE PRESS SYNDICATE OF THE UNIVERSITY OF CAMBRIDGE
The Pitt Building, Trumpington Street, Cambridge, United Kingdom

CAMBRIDGE UNIVERSITY PRESS
The Edinburgh Building, Cambridge CB2 2RU, UK
40 West 20th Street, New York, NY 10011–4211, USA
477 Williamstown Road, Port Melbourne, VIC 3207, Australia
Ruiz de Alarcón 13, 28014 Madrid, Spain
Dock House, The Waterfront, Cape Town 8001, South Africa

http://www.cambridge.org

First published 1999
Third printing 2002

Printed in the United Kingdom at the University Press, Cambridge

Typeset in Tiepolo and Formata

A catalogue record for this book is available from the British Library

ISBN 0 521 59501 0 paperback

Text design by Newton Harris Design Partnership

Map illustration by Kathy Baxendale

ACKNOWLEDGEMENTS
Cover, Hulton Getty; 28, 34, 43, Peter Newark's Pictures; 42, 53, 55, Ullstein
Bilderdienst; 52, Bilderdienst Süddeutscher Verlag; 84, Hulton Deutsch.

The cover photograph of a group of Jews from the Warsaw ghetto being
escorted by German soldiers in 1943 formed part of a report from SS General
Stroop to his commanding officer, and was introduced as evidence to the war
crimes trials in Nuremberg in 1945.

The Holocaust

CAMBRIDGE PERSPECTIVES IN HISTORY
Series editors: Richard Brown and David Smith

Other theme texts in the series include:

The Tudor monarchies, 1485–1603   John McGurk   0 521 59665 3
Authority and disorder in Tudor times, 1485–1603   Paul Thomas   0 521 62664 1
The Renaissance monarchies, 1469–1558   Catherine Mulgan   0 521 59870 2
Papists, Protestants and Puritans, 1559–1714   Diana Newton   0 521 59845 1
British imperialism, 1750–1970   Simon C. Smith   0 521 59930 X
Democracy and the state, 1830–1945   Michael Willis   0 521 59994 6
A disunited kingdom? 1800–1949   Christine Kinealy   0 521 59844 3
Chartism   Richard Brown   0 521 58617 8

Nationalism in Europe, 1789–1945   Timothy Baycroft   0 521 59871 0
Revolutions, 1789–1917   Allan Todd   0 521 58600 3
The origins of the First and Second World Wars   Frank McDonough   0 521 56861 7
Fascism   Richard Thurlow   0 521 59872 9
Hitler and Nazi Germany   Frank McDonough   0 521 59502 9

Contents

Contents

Introduction

Until the early 1960s, according to the historian of the Holocaust Michael Marrus, 'historians outside a small circle of survivors tended to ignore the issue'.[1] This attitude reflected the prevalent incomplete state of knowledge about the events of the Holocaust between 1941 and 1945 (although important documentation was collected during this period), as well as the impact of the Cold War, in Europe. Important documentation on the Holocaust was held by the Soviet Union, and, in the West, European reconstruction seemed to be more important than the pursuit of Nazi war criminals.

An important watershed then occurred with the arrest, trial and execution of the notorious SS killer Adolf Eichmann. In the same year of Eichmann's trial, 1961, Gerald Reitlinger's important book *The 'Final Solution': the attempt to exterminate the Jews of Europe, 1939–45* was published in New York. A new generation of historians subsequently appeared who regarded it as their task to 'integrate the history of the Holocaust into the general stream of historical consciousness'.[2]

The historical debate

The Holocaust has, of course, to be seen against the historical backdrop of European anti-Semitism in earlier centuries, which fed the monstrous racism which we associate with the German Third Reich. Anti-Semitism was not a purely German phenomenon, and this is an important point for students of the Holocaust to remember. Nevertheless, historians have grappled with explanations for the rabid nature of Hitler's anti-Semitism.

Some, indeed – the so-called 'functionalist school', best represented by Martin Broszat and Hans Mommsen – tried to look again at the role of Hitler in the Holocaust and to widen the focus to take in the role of the SS, the Foreign Office, the Economics Ministry and other subordinate Nazi agencies as well. They preferred to see the Nazi slide into genocide as a consequence of a wartime emergency. According to their view, the Nazis were unable to cope with the huge numbers of Jews who fell into their hands between 1939 and 1941 and decided at some point in 1941 to exterminate them. For Mommsen[3] in particular, Hitler was a 'weak dictator': inefficient, although no doubt charismatic, but incapable of formulating a 'blueprint' for the mass murder of the Jews. Nazi Germany, Mommsen believed, was a polycratic empire with rival power centres and leaders, like Göring and Himmler, who competed for the *Führer*'s (the 'leader' –

Hitler's) favours. At a lower level, officials were interpreting a remote *Führer*'s will. Hitler himself, according to Mommsen, had no day-to-day role in the implementation of the Holocaust.

The issue of responsibility

Mommsen's views highlighted one of the central issues involving the Holocaust, that of responsibility. It was his perceived attempt to play down the role of Hitler in initiating the Holocaust which brought a sharp response from another leading historian of the Holocaust, Lucy Dawidowicz. She castigated the functionalists for suggesting that the decisions involving the mass murder of millions of Jews were somehow 'the by-product of the state's structure or functions'[4] and not the responsibility of Hitler and individual Nazi leaders. The net result of such an analysis, Dawidowicz argued, was that human beings were deprived of 'their capacity for good and evil'.[5]

More recently, Daniel Goldhagen[6] has enlarged the debate about Hitler's personal responsibility and that of the regime for the Holocaust to include the whole German people. This analysis sees the death-camp system as exposing 'not just Nazism's but Germany's true face'.[7] According to Goldhagen, whose views were rejected by many historians, ordinary Germans were deeply complicit in Hitler's crimes and could not be exonerated by their claims of ignorance or fear.

The Holocaust deniers

At the extreme end of the historical-debate spectrum have been those mavericks who are broadly described as 'Holocaust deniers'. Michael Marrus has described such people as 'malevolent cranks who contend that the Holocaust never happened'.[8] On this basis, he excludes any discussion of them from his book; a different view would be that they are worthy of mention, if only to highlight the nonsense that they propagate, particularly at a time when fascist-style racism is making a comeback in countries like France and Germany.

The Jewish experience

For someone who is not Jewish, and whose family was not affected by the sheer horror of the Holocaust, it is difficult to address the issue of Jewish suffering and Jewish victimhood. During the last 30 years increasing attention has been paid to the issue of Jewish resistance to the Holocaust, as well as to Jewish suffering. Recent studies, such as those by Yehuda Bauer[9] and Shmuel Krakowski,[10] have highlighted both those traditions which inhibited resistance and the new spirit of resistance which flowed on into the foundation of the Jewish state of Israel in 1948. There are now many published testimonies to individual suffering and heroism in the camps, a notable source being *Can it happen again? Chronicles of the Holocaust*.[11] It could, of course, happen again, as acts of genocide in Cambodia, Bosnia and Rwanda have demonstrated in more recent times.

Finally, neither should we forget (although this book cannot do justice to them) the many thousands of other people – Gypsies, Slavs, homosexuals and Christians, for example – who died in the extermination camps. It was the Nazis' unique concentration on the extermination of the Jewish race in Europe, however, which must form the centrepiece of this study.

Notes and references

1 M. Marrus, *The Holocaust in history*, London, 1987, p. 4.

2 Marrus, *Holocaust in history*, p. xiii.

3 H. Mommsen, 'National socialism: continuity and change', in W. Laqueur, *Fascism: a reader's guide*, Harmondsworth, 1979, p. 180.

4 L. Dawidowicz, *The war against the Jews, 1933–45*, London, 1975, p. xxvi.

5 Dawidowicz, *War against the Jews*, p. xxvi.

6 D. Goldhagen, *Hitler's willing executioners. Ordinary Germans and the Holocaust*, London, 1996.

7 Goldhagen, *Willing executioners*, p. 460.

8 Marrus, *Holocaust in history*, p. xiv.

9 Y. Bauer, *The Jewish emergence from powerlessness*, Toronto, 1979.

10 S. Krakowski, *The war of the doomed: Jewish armed resistance in Poland, 1942–44*, New York, 1984.

11 R. K. Chartock and J. Spencer (eds.), New York, 1995.

Anti-Semitism in European and German history

This chapter will deal with three major issues.

1 The growth of anti-Jewish prejudice in Europe and its intellectual origins.
2 The specific role of such prejudice in modern German history and the extent to which a study of its roots helps to explain the appearance of the historical phenomenon known as 'national socialism'.
3 Hitler's personal anti-Semitism.

The first point to make, and it is an important one, is that any study of the Nazi persecution of the Jews during the 1930s and 1940s does not depend upon 'claims that anti-Jewish ideology was a predominantly German doctrine or a constant preoccupation of the leaders of the Third Reich'.[1] Anti-Semitism was not the sole preserve of the German people; it was as old as European civilisation itself.

The religious dimension

The harsh, historical fate of the Jewish people was linked to two crucial events: the first was the crucifixion and death of Jesus Christ in AD 33 and the second was the failure of the Jewish uprising against the Roman Empire from AD 69 to AD 70.

The first event placed the historical burden upon the Jews of the accusation of having been the murderers of Christ, the Messiah whom they refused to accept (in Judaism the Messiah is regarded as the 'chosen one', sent by God to save the Jewish people). The second event destroyed the kingdom of Israel as the Romans exacted their revenge on the Jews, forcing them to flee to every part of the known world. This 'Diaspora', or scattering, of the Jews would mean that they would not have a country which they could call their own again until 1948, when the modern state of Israel was founded.

Following the Diaspora, the history of the Jews was a melancholy one, for they became targeted for persecution throughout Christian Europe. In England, for example, there were massacres of Jews in London and York in 1263 and 1290 respectively, while in Germany Crusaders on their way to fight the Islamic Turks in the Holy Land (Palestine) massacred Jews in the Rhineland cities; in France anti-Jewish prejudice resulted in the confiscation of all Jewish property in 1306. Such massacres (and the theft of Jewish property) were frequently justified by the claim that the Jews were the 'enemies' of Christ.

Religious observance also contributed to another traditional Christian prejudice against the Jews – that they were unscrupulous moneylenders (the Catholic Church decreed that usury, that is lending money at interest, was a sin). Rulers during the medieval period clearly needed to raise money for administrative and military purposes, but the only effective moneylenders available were the Jews. Because they fulfilled this function, which Christians could not, Jews were hated and reviled.

Matters got even worse for the Jews when the Reformation began in the early part of the sixteenth century. The German theological reformer Martin Luther (1483–1546) was strongly anti-Semitic during the early stages of his career, so that although his followers, the Protestants (as they became known), attacked the alleged abuses in the Catholic Church, they were not friends of the Jews. A rare beacon of tolerance shone out in England, however, when, in 1656, Oliver Cromwell, the Lord Protector of the Commonwealth, allowed the Jews to resettle there after their expulsion from the country in the thirteenth century.

The Enlightenment

In the eighteenth century there was an atmosphere of religious scepticism in many parts of Europe as a result of the so-called 'Enlightenment'. Its leading thinkers, like Voltaire (1694–1778) and Jean Jacques Rousseau (1712–78), were critical of the Christian churches and preached the need for personal liberty and equality before the law. This was intended to include equality of treatment for the Jews, too, but the ideals of the Enlightenment, which were strongly evident in France after the revolution of 1789, actually produced something of a nationalistic backlash in countries like Spain, Germany and Russia. (Progressive thinking was associated with France, but between 1792 and 1814 the French dominated Europe, often in an oppressive way.) Nevertheless, the Jews gained from the removal of anti-Semitic restrictions in French-occupied Italy and Germany.

State-sponsored anti-Semitism

At the end of the nineteenth century a disturbing development took place in Russia, when the Tsarist government actually encouraged attacks on the Jews. Between 1880 and the outbreak of the First World War in 1914 there were numerous 'pogroms' (the word today generally used for anti-Jewish atrocities) and Jews were officially excluded from many areas of normal life. (One result of this anti-Semitic persecution was that many young Jews, Leon Trotsky and Grigori Zinoviev among them, joined revolutionary groups like the Bolshevik Party.)

The worst anti-Semitic outbreak took place in Kishinev in 1903, when, for two days, the local population was allowed to attack Jews (as a result of which 50 people died) without interference from the police or army. The tsar, Nicholas II, was a known anti-Semite, like his father, Alexander III, and he, too, failed to intervene. Ten years later, in 1913, the notorious Beilis case occurred, when a young Jew was accused of murdering a child in order to obtain Christian blood for one of the alleged, secret rituals in which Jews were accused of taking part. This was also the time when the 'Protocols of the Elders of Zion' emerged in Russia, a forged document which claimed that the Jews were conspiring to take over the world.

A clear message was therefore being sent from Russia, which was to have strong echoes in twentieth-century Europe.

1 Jews were supposedly 'alien' and not part of the nation (in Russia they were forced to leave the cities and live in designated areas).
2 Their very presence was allegedly a threat to the 'ethnic purity' of the nation.

The Dreyfus case

The pervasiveness of anti-Semitism in Europe was demonstrated during the 1890s in the notorious Dreyfus case in France, generally regarded as the most cultivated nation in Europe. In this instance, a Jewish army officer, Alfred Dreyfus (who also happened to be an Alsatian – Alsace was a region of France which was under German rule at that time), was accused of spying for Germany. Dreyfus was dismissed from the French army in 1894 and was sent to the penal colony of Devil's Island in French Guyana. In the end, Dreyfus was found to be an innocent man and was restored to his position in the army in 1906, but his case divided the nation. The political right – the army's high command and the Catholic Church – had been all too willing to condemn Dreyfus because he was a Jew and therefore supposedly not truly French (as it turned out, the real spy was not Jewish). At least Dreyfus ultimately obtained justice, something that many of his race were denied by the anti-Semitic excesses and hatred of the twentieth century.

German anti-Semitism

The point about anti-Semitism being a European-wide phenomenon is an important one, but it still leaves the historical difficulty of explaining why German anti-Semitism during the Nazi period was so brutal and intolerant. The difference between the unpleasant and random persecution of a Jewish individual, such as Dreyfus, and the deliberately planned deaths of 6 million Jews in Nazi death camps is plainly enormous.

Anti-Semitism had been strong in Germany since the Reformation. Luther had established the Protestant Church in Germany, but in another sense he also became the 'father' of German anti-Semitism. Germany also reacted against the freedoms advocated by the French Revolution, which included equality for Jews.

This inherent German conservatism and prejudice was most strongly represented by the German philosopher Johann Gottlieb Fichte (1762–1814) at the end of the eighteenth century, who denied that Jews were entitled to equality; he also described the Jews as being essentially 'alien' and therefore likely to undermine the German nation. The only way to deal with Jews, argued Fichte, was 'to cut off all their heads in one night, and to set new ones on their shoulders, which should contain not a single Jewish idea'.[2] Like most German anti-Semites, Fichte was convinced of the superiority of German culture. The ideas of the French Revolution, focusing on liberty, equality and fraternity, were, Fichte believed, a threat to German culture and nationhood. He held these ideas even though Germany was then a ramshackle collection of states, the largest of which was Prussia. One of the implications of Germany's fragmentation was that being German at that time was defined in cultural and ethnic terms: there was no German state as such, so Germans defined themselves in terms of their German *Volk* (race), language and culture.

German unity

The national unification of Germany was achieved under Prussian leadership after the Franco-Prussian War of 1870–71. A 'nation' which had previously been defined by a shared language and culture was thus now recognised as having national boundaries and a place in the European national family.

Germans remained curiously insecure after the unification of their country, however, even though the new German *Reich* (empire) was the strongest industrial and military power in Europe.

Anti-Semitism and the political right

This insecurity was largely a characteristic of the German political right, as was the hatred of Jews. The German social-democratic leader August Bebel famously remarked that anti-Semitism was the 'socialism of fools' and that the political left did not need such a primitive prejudice. (It had its own, sophisticated, political-belief system in Marxism, the philosophical-political system developed by Karl Marx (1818–83) and Friedrich Engels (1820–95); anti-Semitic rightists were quick to point out the fact that Marx, the father of world communism, was a Jew.)

By the 1890s, anti-Semitism was a potent force in the new Germany. This was partly a reaction to the rise of social democracy (by 1914 the Social Democratic Party (*Sozialdemokratische Partei Deutschlands*, SPD) was the largest party in the Reichstag, the German parliament), which was, perhaps inevitably, linked with Judaism. German anti-Semitism was also a result of age-old Protestant prejudice against the Jews, however (and the influence of Luther should therefore be noted here). Anti-Semites tended to be Protestant members of the *Mittelstand* (middle class), although during the Nazi period some of the most virulent racists were Austrian Catholics, like Hitler. These members of the middle class were alarmed by the rise of working-class power through the SPD and looked for easy scapegoats for their anxieties, finding them in the Jews (as always, irrational fear and hysteria played its part in anti-Semitism). By 1914, some 90 anti-Semitic members of the political centre-right had been elected to the Reichstag. Their success also reflected the fact that Jews had a dominant position in German banking and finance houses, which was resented in German society (as illustrated by an unpleasant attack on the German chancellor, Otto von Bismarck's, Jewish personal banker, Gerson Blechröder, in 1875 by a conservative newspaper).

Leading anti-Semites

Nineteenth-century anti-Semites in Germany tended to be more obsessed with race and less concerned with Christianity than their predecessors. Among them were Karl Dühring, a member of the right-wing German Reform Party; Wilhelm Marr (who described Christianity as a 'disease of consciousness'); and Adolf Stöcker, who founded the Christian Social Workers' Party. Such men were heavily influenced by the essay by the French racial theorist Arthur de Gobineau (1816–82) on the inequality of races, published during the 1850s, which argued that race was the key factor in the rise and fall of nation states. Another influence on them was the famous German composer Richard Wagner (1813–83), a ferocious anti-Semite who looked back to a pre-Christian, mythical Germany free of Jews and the home of flaxen-haired heroes and heroines, who frequently appeared in his operas. Wagner's son-in-law was the Englishman Houston Chamberlain, who wrote the influential work *Foundations of the nineteenth century*, another key anti-Semitic text.

Gobineau, Wagner and Chamberlain, in particular, all contributed to the concept of racial superiority as being an inbred characteristic that was an essential component of Nazism. Yet the anti-Semitism of the 1890s also owed a good deal to the complex insecurities of the extreme political right, which would also feed into national socialism after the First World War. Anti-Semites were often worshippers of the outdoors, food-faddists and occultists; they were also, like the Nazis, almost invariably extreme nationalists. The Pan-German League, for example, which had been set up in 1893 to campaign for the creation of a German empire and the associated unification of all ethnic Germans living in Europe, was clearly anti-Jewish by 1908: Jews were excluded from its membership. The same exclusion was true of the National Germanic League of Clerks, dating from 1893, and the Agrarian League. All these fringe lobby groups regarded Jews as being both 'alien' and wielding too much influence in Germany (anti-Semitic propaganda always exaggerated the degree to which Jews dominated the professions).

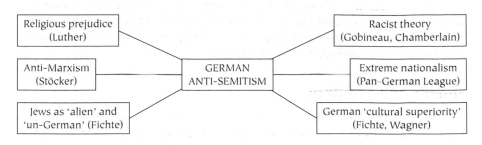

Figure 1. The roots of German anti-Semitism.

The impact of the First World War

The war of 1914 to 1918 is recognised by historians as having been a crucial component in the development of German post-war fascism, or Nazism. In 1914, on the outbreak of war, there was an outburst of extreme patriotism as all loyal Germans were encouraged to rally around the national flag. This *Burgfrieden* ('truce') spirit of 1914 between the political left and right initially included the Jews, but when Germany began to lose the war anti-Jewish prejudice was revived (the fact that 12,000 German Jews gave their lives for the 'Fatherland' was all too easily forgotten).

The Bolshevik Revolution of 1917 in Russia furthermore created a sinister link in the minds of right-wing German nationalists between Judaism and communism (it was undeniably true that some Bolshevik leaders, like Trotsky and Zinoviev, were Jewish). The lie that Jews were somehow profiting financially from the war also proved to be attractive to the right-wing nationalists.

The biggest anti-Semitic lie of all, propagated at the end of the First World War, became particularly potent in right-wing circles This was the *Dolchstoss-legende* (the stab-in-the-back legend), which claimed that Jews had somehow betrayed Germany by fomenting revolution when the German army was winning the war. Individual Jews, like Walter Rathenau (a future foreign minister of the post-war Weimar Republic), were made somehow responsible for the German Revolution of 1918, when, in fact, most of its leaders were not Jewish. This was nonsense, as Germany's military leaders, Erich Ludendorff and Paul von Hindenburg, well knew: the German army had been defeated by the Allied powers, but Germany's war lords, who had effectively been running the country since 1916, could not bring themselves to admit it. The legend of the *Dolchstoss* would be the most potent of all the right-wing, nationalist myths during the post-war period. It increased the impact of historical German anti-Semitism and encouraged the spawning of a number of far-right political parties, of which the NSDAP (*Nationalsozialistische Deutsche Arbeiterpartei*, the National Socialist German Workers' Party), soon to be led by Adolf Hitler, was one.

Another important point about the First World War in relation to anti-Semitism was that it produced a generation of disillusioned former soldiers who rejected Germany's post-war democracy as effete and corrupt. These men, who almost invariably found their way into the racist, political right, identified the Jews as a 'cancer' in the body politic. Only when the Jews and their communist allies were neutralised, they believed, could the shame and defeat of 1918 be avenged. One of these former soldiers, who was recovering from being gassed in France when the war ended, was Adolf Hitler.

Hitler's anti-Semitism

Adolf Hitler was born in Austria in 1889. This fact is in itself highly significant, for the young Hitler was a citizen of the Austro-Hungarian Empire. It was an empire which had traditionally been dominated by the Austrian Germans before becoming the so-called 'Dual Monarchy' in 1867. It was also a hotchpotch of different races, however, most of which (such as the Poles, Czechs, Slovaks, Ruthenes and Croats) were Slavs. Ethnic Germans, one of whom was Hitler's own father, Alois, tended to look down on the Slavs as being 'racially inferior'. This feeling of superiority was even more pronounced in the case of the Jews, even though some of the most powerful and influential families in the empire were Jewish (the most notable being the Rothschilds, a famous banking dynasty). In the minds of anti-Semites, such Jewish success seemed proof of the Jews' alleged traditional manipulation of the empire's financial resources.

The young Hitler

Hitler's family background was complicated. His father married three times and Adolf was the fourth child of his third wife, Klara, who was 23 years younger than Alois. Hitler had several half-brothers and half-sisters as a result of Alois Hitler's serial marital experience.

More pertinently, and intriguingly, there is some mystery about Hitler's paternal grandfather: according to one version, attributed to Hitler's cousin, William Patrick Hitler, his grandfather may have been Jewish, but this allegation is almost certainly without foundation. Nevertheless, as one leading historian of the Holocaust has pointed out, 'uncertainties about his own ancestry must have obsessed the man who made ancestry the measure of the Aryan [those of Germanic race] man'.[3]

When Adolf was five the family left its home in Braunau-am-Inn, on the Austro-German border, and moved to Leonding, a suburb of the city of Linz. Hitler was not a success at school and was described later by one of his teachers as being 'notoriously cantankerous, wilful, arrogant and bad tempered'.[4] He never took his final examinations and thus never received a secondary-school diploma. His relationship with his father, who died in 1903, was tense and acrimonious. Young Adolf seems to have been a typical teenage rebel: he wanted to become an artist, whereas Alois Hitler wanted his son to go into business or to have a technical career. Unfortunately for Hitler, and, in the long run, the whole of Europe, he lacked the talent to become a professional painter.

Hitler's schooldays seem to have been significant only in the sense that he developed a life-long inferiority complex about his lack of formal educational qualifications, as well as an abiding hatred of 'professors'. Only his history master at secondary school is selected for praise in Hitler's book, *Mein Kampf* ('My struggle'), and Hitler, characteristically, got his name wrong!

We look in vain to Hitler's early years for an explanation of his later extreme anti-Semitism, although a recent, controversial study may throw light on it. This book, *The Jew of Linz*, by Kimberley Cornish,[5] suggests that the 'one Jewish boy' referred to by Hitler in *Mein Kampf* was, in fact, Ludwig Wittgenstein, later a famous philosopher at Cambridge University during the 1930s. Wittgenstein was the son of extremely wealthy, Viennese Jews (his father became one of the greatest industrialists in the Austro-Hungarian Empire) and Hitler might well have envied such material success, which contrasted sharply with his own, relatively humble, origins. It has to be acknowledged, however, that Hitler and

Wittgenstein's schooldays overlapped only in the academic year of 1904 to 1905, and that Cornish perhaps sets too much store by a photograph of the schoolboy Hitler at Linz, with Wittgenstein appearing in a row below him.

The idea that Hitler's anti-Semitism evolved from his dislike of Wittgenstein is a fascinating one. But most historians have dated the origins of Hitler's anti-Semitism to his early manhood and have generally been at a loss to explain its virulence. Ultimately, as Ian Kershaw has pointed out, in his biography of Hitler, 'we remain in the dark about why Hitler became a manic anti-Semite'.[6]

The evolution of Hitler's anti-Semitism

In the absence of any convincing support for Cornish's theory, it seems safer to accept the more conventional view: that Hitler's anti-Semitism dates from a later period. The traditional view, that Hitler's anti-Semitic obsession derived from the period that he spent in Vienna after 1908, has recently been challenged. In her book *Hitler's Vienna*, Brigitte Hamann suggests that Hitler only became a convinced anti-Semite after the First World War. She points out that Hitler went to Jewish parties and mixed with Jews in his decrepit lodging-house. In 1952, too, Alan Bullock referred in his biography, *Hitler. A study in tyranny*,[7] to the relationship between the aspiring artist, Hitler, and the Jew Neumann, who befriended him in the doss-house.

Hitler continued to be a failure in Vienna. He failed to get into either the art academy or the architectural academy and became a restless drifter who was dependent on a small family legacy. He read voraciously, if unsystematically, went to the opera a good deal and imposed his increasingly right-wing ideas on those who would listen to him in working-men's hostels. Hitler the demagogue was in the process of being born.

At this juncture it should be pointed out that anti-Semitism was endemic in Vienna when Hitler was living there between 1908 and 1913 and that it therefore influenced Hitler at this time. But the more modern view is that in *Mein Kampf* Hitler overstated his anti-Jewish prejudice in this early part of his life. Hitler reflected the prejudices of those in the Viennese working and middle classes who tended to support right-wing parties before 1914. Before he came to Vienna, on his own admission, Hitler knew few Jews, yet by the time he left the city, in 1913, for Germany, Hitler was aware of the writings of virulent anti-Semites, even though he may not then have been a convinced anti-Semite himself.

Historians still remain in the dark for an explanation of his pathological hatred of a people who had never done him or his family any personal harm. The extreme nature of Hitler's subsequent anti-Semitism is demonstrated in the following passage, one of many which could have been selected from Hitler's writings.

Was there any shady undertaking, any form of foulness, especially in cultural life, in which at least one Jew did not participate? On putting the probing knife carefully to that kind of abscess one immediately discovered, like a maggot in a putrescent body, a little Jew who was often blinded by the sudden light.[8]

For Hitler, the Jew was a creature of the night, waiting to pollute the German race.

Some so-called 'psycho-historians' have sought an explanation for Hitler's racism in his sexuality. His constant references to Jews as 'seducers' of 'innocent German maidens' have suggested that Hitler may have contracted syphilis in his youth or have undergone an unfortunate sexual experience. Alternatively, Hitler's difficult relationship with his father, or his key relationship with his mother, Klara, have been blamed for his latent, obsessive racism. Klara died in 1907, and the family doctor, Dr Bloch, reported that 'In all my career, I never saw anyone so prostrate with grief as Adolf Hitler'.[9] Was Hitler, as some have suggested, full of guilt because of his feckless lifestyle, his academic failure and his arrival home when his mother was on her deathbed (his first visit to Vienna was just before Klara Hitler's death)? There will probably never be a satisfactory explanation for Hitler's manic anti-Semitism. What is beyond doubt, however, are its consequences.

Hitler the soldier

The personality patterns which were laid down in Vienna re-emerged when Hitler joined the German army in 1914 (he had avoided conscription into the Austro-Hungarian army). The war gave Hitler the cause that he had been looking for and he appears to have been a brave enough soldier, winning the Iron Cross, First Class. In the army, he subjected his comrades to his anti-Jewish, anti-Slavic and anti-socialist rantings, which makes the point that the Jews were not the only victims of Hitler's prejudices. Nevertheless, army life seems to have given Hitler the comradeship and security that he craved.

The German military collapse in the autumn of 1918 came as a shock to Hitler. Unable to accept the defeat of his adopted country, Hitler sought refuge in fantasy. The Jews, he believed, were to blame for the downfall of his beloved 'Fatherland' and, years later, when Hitler had supreme power in Germany, he determined that if he were to be defeated in a European war the Jews would be made to pay.

Ironically, it was the army that gave Hitler his entry into far-right politics. When he was asked to report on the activities of the newly formed German Workers' Party (*Deutsche Arbeiterpartei*, DAP) in 1919, Hitler was so impressed by what he heard that he decided to join the party instead (it soon changed its name to the National Socialist German Workers' Party). He now had a platform for his racism and his xenophobia.

The origins of anti-Semitism

1.1 Luther's influence on anti-Semitism

Know Christian, that next to the devil thou hast no enemy more cruel, more venomous and violent than a true Jew.

Source: L. Dawidowicz, *The war against the Jews, 1933–45*, London, 1975, p. 50

1.2 Anti-Semitism as a European phenomenon: the Dreyfus case

Above all Dreyfus was a Jew. The fact that he was Jewish, Marcel Thomas has observed, played no role at the beginning of the Affair . . . But from the moment his name was mentioned by d'Abboville . . . the fact that he was a Jew became – complementary or conclusive – grounds for presuming his guilt.

Source: J. D. Bredin, *The affair. The case of Alfred Dreyfus*, London, 1987, p. 533

1.3 Viennese anti-Semitism

Are You Blond? Then You Are A Culture-Creator
And A Culture Supporter!
Are You Blond? If so, danger threatens you!

Source: the anti-Semitic magazine *Ostara*, Vienna, 1900s

1.4 Hitler's first encounter with a Viennese Jew

One day when passing through the Inner City, I suddenly encountered a phenomenon in a long caftan and wearing black sidelocks. My first thought was: is this a Jew? They certainly did not have this appearance in Linz, I watched the man stealthily and cautiously, but the longer I gazed at this strange countenance and examined it section by section, the more the question shaped itself in my brain: is this a German? I turned to my books for help in removing my doubts. For the first time in my life I bought myself some anti-Semitic pamphlets for a few pence.

Source: A. Hitler, *Mein Kampf*, Munich, 1925, p. 59

1.5 Germany, 1918: the trauma of defeat

The situation of the German army by November 1918 was in fact without hope. It was only a matter of time before it was driven back into Germany and destroyed. Yet, at the moment when the German Government signed the capitulation, the German army still stood outside Germany's frontiers and still preserved an unbroken front in the west. Moreover, although the initiative for ending the war had come from the High Command, from General Ludendorff himself, this fact was concealed. The High Command not only left the civil government, hitherto denied any voice in the conduct of the war, to take the full responsibility for ending it, but tried to dissociate itself from the consequences of the decision.

Source: A. Bullock, *Hitler. A study in tyranny*, revised edn, London, 1962, pp. 57–58

1 Briefly describe Luther's attitude to the Jews, referred to in 1.1.

2 What grounds are presented in 1.2 for assuming the guilt of Alfred Dreyfus?

3 How helpful are 1.1, 1.2 and 1.3 as historical sources for explaining the phenomenon of European anti-Semitism?

4 What light does 1.4 throw on the origins of Hitler's personal anti-Semitism?

5 What link can be established between Hitler's comments in 1.4 and the events described in 1.5?

Notes and references

1 M. Marrus, *The Holocaust in history*, London, 1987, p. 8.

2 L. Dawidowicz, *The war against the Jews, 1933–45*, London, 1975, p. 54.

3 Dawidowicz, *War against the Jews*, p. 30.

4 A. Bullock, *Hitler. A study in tyranny*, revised edn, London, 1962, p. 27.

5 K. Cornish, *The Jew of Linz*, London, 1998.

6 I. Kershaw, *Hitler*, London, 1991, p. 19.

7 Bullock, *Hitler*, pp. 34–36.

8 A. Hitler, *Mein Kampf*, translation by James Murphy, London, 1939, p. 60.

9 J. Tolland, *Adolf Hitler*, New York, 1976, p. 27.

2 Anti-Semitism and the rise of the Nazi Party

Adolf Hitler soon became prominent in the affairs of the German Workers' Party (DAP) after he joined it in 1919. It was Hitler, along with the party leader, Anton Drexler, who drew up the DAP's 25-point programme in February 1920. Point 4 in this programme stated that 'Only members of the *Volk* [German people] may be citizens of the State. Only those of German blood, whatever their creed may be members of the nation. Accordingly no Jew may be a member of the nation.' Anti-Semitic racism was thus a central part of Nazi thinking from the outset. (The DAP changed its name to the National Socialist Workers' Party (NSDAP, or Nazi Party) in April 1920 and Hitler became its leader in 1921.) This chapter will analyse its importance during the Nazi Party's rise to power between 1919 and 1933.

The rise of the racist right

Initially, the Nazi Party was only one of a number of extreme right-wing parties in Germany, whose defining characteristics were anti-Semitism and anti-communism. Such right-wing nationalists accused the new, democratic Weimar Republic (established in 1918) of betraying Germany by signing the Treaty of Versailles in 1919 (in reality it had no choice). They also attacked it for allowing Jews to occupy important positions in the government.

The myth of the 'Jewish–Bolshevik conspiracy' occupied a central place in the thinking of German right-wing, nationalist fanatics. It was in this atmosphere that the Jewish foreign minister, Walter Rathenau, was assassinated by a right-wing paramilitary squad in 1922. The right-wing *Freikorps* ('free corps' – a right-wing, paramilitary force) had also murdered the Jewish communist Rosa Luxemburg and Karl Liebknecht, the leaders of the Spartacists, after a failed uprising in Berlin in 1919.

However, it was not just extreme-right eccentrics, like Hitler and Drexler, who were seduced by anti-Semitic rhetoric: the supposedly respectable German National People's Party (*Deutschnationale Volkspartei*, DNVP) had also become anti-Semitic by 1920. Across Germany, there was a vast increase in anti-Semitic activity: by 1933 there were over 400 anti-Semitic associations and societies and as many as 700 anti-Jewish periodicals. There were also constant attempts on the part of the anti-Semitic political right to introduce anti-Jewish laws into both the Reichstag and the legislatures of states like Bavaria and Prussia. Perhaps most worrying for supporters of democracy and tolerance in Germany was the fact that university students in particular were strongly anti-Semitic (in student elections in Berlin in 1921 two-thirds of the vote was given to anti-Semitic candidates). At the same time, the notorious anti-Semitic forgery the 'Protocols of the Elders of Zion', a product of Russian anti-Semitism, became a best-seller in Germany.

German politics, 1919–24

The growth of German anti-Semitism took place against a backdrop of extreme political and economic instability. The infant Weimar Republic was under attack from both the political right and left during its early years, and was also struggling to meet the massive reparations bill imposed upon Germany by the Treaty of Versailles to compensate the victors of the First World War. In 1921 the Allied powers agreed on the final figure – Germany was to pay £6,600 million in compensation for having started the First World War and for the damage done by its army during the war. Germans also bitterly resented Article 231 of the Treaty of Versailles, the 'war-guilt clause', in which it was stated that Germany had to accept responsibility for starting the war.

The most dangerous period for the Weimar Republic came between 1918 and 1919. There were two communist uprisings – in Berlin (that of the Spartacists) and Bavaria – which attempted to set up Russian-style Soviet republics in Germany. In Munich, the capital of Bavaria, the attempted communist *Putsch* (*coup d'état*) was led by a Jew, Kurt Eisner, and a murderous revenge was taken by the local *Freikorps* on Eisner and his communist supporters. In the following year, 1920, a right-wing *Putsch* in Berlin, led by Wolfgang Kapp, was crushed by a combination of a workers' general strike and the refusal of the army's leaders to support Kapp.

The year of 1923 was a traumatic one for the Weimar government. In January, French and Belgian troops occupied the Ruhr, Germany's main industrial region, when Germany defaulted on some of its reparations payments. The German response to this was to organise 'peaceful' resistance to French rule, which in turn led to a closedown of the Ruhr's steelmills and coalmines. The combination of such industrial paralysis and the economic pressure of reparations caused massive inflation and the collapse of the German currency, the mark: millions of marks might only buy a worker a box of matches.

Hitler's 'beerhall *Putsch*'

This was the background to the attempted *Putsch* by Adolf Hitler and the Nazi Party between 8 and 9 November 1923. Hitler had enlisted the help of the old war hero Ludendorff in his attempt to seize power in Bavaria, and he also hoped for the support of the local army and political leaders.

Hitler had been attempting to make links with the Bavarian army's commander, General Otto von Lossow, since March 1923, using rhetoric that was typical of his anti-Semitic tirades of the pre-1933 period. According to Hitler, the Jews ran the Weimar Republic, which was a corrupt government which undermined

Germany's national interests; they were the so-called 'November criminals' who had signed the ceasefire in 1918. The last accusation was, in fact, quite untrue, as the German government had been represented at the armistice of November 1918 by a Catholic Centre Party politician, Matthias Erzberger (he, too, was subsequently gunned down by a right-wing paramilitary squad).

In the event, Hitler's *Putsch* was a fiasco. Von Lossow would not support the overthrow of the governments in either Munich or Berlin and neither would local Bavarian politicians. Hitler and his followers, including Ludendorff, were fired on by the police while marching through Munich's city centre and dispersed in confusion. Hitler was arrested shortly afterwards.

Hitler's trial

Hitler's trial was a farce. He had committed treason against the German state by planning to overthrow it but he was sentenced to five years' imprisonment only, of which he served just nine months in Landsberg prison. During his trial, a sympathetic judge allowed him to harangue the court with his anti-Semitic and extreme nationalist opinions (thereby illustrating the point that the judiciary in Weimar Germany was generally consistently right-wing in its attitudes). 'There is no such thing as high treason against the traitors of 1918', Hitler told the court, and he went on to tell it how, when he 'stood for the first time at the grave of Richard Wagner [the anti-Semitic composer] my heart overflowed with pride'.[1] Hitler had defied the Weimar democracy and got away with it.

The writing of *Mein Kampf*

It was during his short period in prison that Hitler began to write *Mein Kampf* (his publisher advised him to drop the original title, 'Four-and-a-half years of struggle against lies, stupidity and cowardice', in favour of 'My struggle'). This became the core text of the Nazi movement and therefore a key anti-Semitic text as well.

Hitler was anxious to establish his credentials as an 'intellectual', as several other prominent Nazis, including Alfred Rosenberg and Gottfried Feder, had written political books and pamphlets. He wrote *Mein Kampf* over the period 1924–25, a period which also encompassed his release from Landsberg prison and his resumption of the leadership of the Nazi Party (during which he had to deal with a number of petty internal disputes within the Nazi Party, which had been, and remained, fractious).

His book was a vehicle for Hitler's ferocious anti-Semitism. After describing the time that he spent in hospital at the end of the First World War, Hitler ended the chapter by saying that 'We cannot bargain with Jews, only present them with a hard "either-or"'.[2] Then, explaining how he had decided to become a political leader, Hitler stated that it would be his task to solve the 'Jewish question' by radical and brutal means. 'Therefore I am now convinced', Hitler wrote, 'that I am acting as the agent of our Creator by fighting off the Jews, I am doing the Lord's work.'[3] This statement can be regarded as blatant hypocrisy, as Hitler regarded Christianity as a creed for the weak and submissive and had long abandoned the Catholicism of his boyhood. There were, however, anti-Semites in the Christian churches who were impressed by Hitler's religious nonsense as presented in *Mein Kampf*, with its leavening of extreme nationalism and anti-communism.

Mein Kampf is a turgid and badly written book – the work, in fact, of a half-educated man who had failed to obtain a secondary-school diploma. Nevertheless, the text gives crucial insights into Hitler's thinking and the genesis of his anti-Semitism.

The lean years

During the years between 1924 and 1928 the Nazi Party was a failure in electoral terms: in the 1928 Reichstag elections it obtained just 12 seats in parliament and a popular vote of only 800,000 across Germany (even though the Weimar proportional-representation system favoured fringe parties like the NSDAP). It is therefore clear that although the Nazis tried to peddle their anti-Semitic propaganda to the German electorate anti-Semitism was not a vote-winner. Improved economic circumstances in Germany were clearly making political extremism less attractive in the eyes of the electorate.

The Nazis did, however, have some success with their anti-Semitic rhetoric in agrarian areas of Germany, indulging in their usual crude distortion of facts. One example of this strategy, given by the historian W. S. Allen,[4] concerns an attempt by the Nazis in the town of Northeim to claim that the local Jewish rabbi was using cruel slaughtering methods on local animals. Local Nazis were observed by newspaper reporters hanging around the slaughterhouse and abusing local Jews; a member of the Social Democratic Party then brought a case against a Nazi newspaper for using the headline 'Gruesome torture of animals at the Northeim slaughterhouse'. This sort of crude sensationalism, reminiscent of the propagation of age-old myths about Jews supposedly drinking Christian children's blood during ritual sacrifices, conspicuously failed to attract votes. A poll of Nazi Party members during this period showed that, even amongst this group, only 13.6 per cent of them regarded anti-Semitism as being a crucial issue, whereas almost two-thirds were anti-communist.

Hitler was a fanatic, but he could also be pragmatic: faced with the fact that the NSDAP's anti-Semitism did not seem to be attracting the votes of the German electorate, he consequently played it down. He was also astute enough to use anti-Semitism for his own electoral purposes. When challenged by the radical wing of the Nazi Party which was hostile to big business and capitalist interests, for example, Hitler allowed it verbally to attack the Jewish owners of big department stores and Jewish bankers. Because Hitler needed the support of big industrialists, like the Krupp family (which was not Jewish), he allowed Nazi propagandists to attack Jewish capitalists only. This strategy had the desirable consequence for Hitler of pleasing the NSDAP's radical, anti-capitalist wing, led by Gregor Strasser, while at the same time maintaining Nazi contacts with big business. Hitler's pragmatism therefore meant that 'Nazi propaganda did not make anti-Semitism a primary issue in its final, opportunistic drive for electoral power'.[5]

The Nazi achievement of power

The relegation of anti-Semitic propaganda to a lesser position in the Nazi Party's priorities continued as the Nazis began to pile up the votes after the Reichstag election of 1930, when they secured the election of 107 deputies. Historians agree that the Nazis gained political ground as a result of the world-wide economic depression which followed the Wall Street Crash of 1929 in the USA. This meant that the short-term US loans granted by the Dawes Plan (and subsequently the Young Plan from 1929) in order to help Germany out of financial difficulty in 1924 were called in, causing the German economy to plunge into recession. By 1932 6 million Germans were out of work.

This desperate economic situation was ripe for exploitation by Hitler and his propaganda expert, Joseph Goebbels. The Nazis had never had much success in winning votes from either the industrial working class or Catholics, but now Hitler's message was pitched in a manner which was attractive to many sections of German society. Hitler promised rearmament to the army generals, economic stability to the bankers, employment to the unemployed and the revision of the Treaty of Versailles to German nationalists. As he was a brilliant orator, many were seduced by his message. For their part, many of Germany's 525,000 Jews believed that once the Nazis were in power they might curb their anti-Semitism and adopt more moderate policies; this misconception arose from Hitler's short-term pragmatism, which disguised the virulence of his anti-Semitism in the years between 1929 and 1933.

When the Nazis came to power, in January 1933, they did so through the back door. Their share of the vote had fallen in the Reichstag elections of November 1932 (only 196 seats were won, compared to 230 in July). They were also running out of the money required to fund Hitler's highly expensive election campaigns (there were two presidential campaigns in 1932, which Hitler lost to von Hindenburg). As Goebbels' diaries show, the Nazis were becoming anxious and dispirited. They were saved, however, by the foolishness of the former German chancellor, Franz von Papen, who believed that Hitler could be used as a stooge by the right-wing, conservative clique which surrounded the aged President von Hindenburg. Von Papen, who needed Hitler's electoral appeal because he had no popular support himself, persuaded the old president to make Hitler chancellor of Germany on 30 January 1933, upon which he announced 'We've hired Hitler'. Millions of Jews and other minority peoples in Europe would pay for von Papen's folly.

Anti-Semitism and the Nazi rise to power

2.1 Right-wing racism in 1920s' Germany

Knallt ab den Walter Rathenau
Die gottverdammte Judensau.
['Mow down Walter Rathenau
The goddammed Jewish sow.']

Source: L. Dawidowicz, *The war against the Jews, 1933–45*, London, 1975, p. 77

2.2 Nazi anti-Semitism

Point 4. Only members of the *Volk* [German people] may be citizens of the State. Only those of German blood, whatever their creed may be members of the nation. Accordingly no Jew may be a member of the nation.

Source: the Nazi Party programme, 1920, quoted in G. Layton, *Germany: the Third Reich*, London, 1992, p. 17

2.3 Hitler's anti-Semitic beliefs

The final Jewish goal is denationalization, is sowing confusion by the bastardization of other nations, lowering the racial level of the highest, and dominating this racial stew by exterminating the folkish intelligentsias and replacing them by members of his own race . . . Just as he himself [the Jew] systematically ruins women and girls, he does not shrink back from pulling down the blood barriers from others, even on a large scale.

Source: A. Hitler, *Mein Kampf*, Munich, 1925, p. 325

2.4 The 'Jewish–Bolshevik conspiracy'

It is by no means settled that the capitalist and the Bolshevik Jew are one and the same. The Jewish Question is more complicated than one imagines.

Source: Joseph Goebbels, 1926

2.5 Von Papen's view of Hitler

When Edwald von Kleist-Schmenzin, a conservative Prussian Junker aristocrat who would later lose his life for opposing Hitler's dictatorship, protested against Papen's scheme that same day, the latter's rejoinder was 'What do you want? I have the confidence of Hindenburg. In two months we'll have pushed Hitler so far into a corner that he'll squeal'.

Source: Henry Ashby Turner Jr., *Hitler's thirty days to power, January 1933*, London, 1997, p. 147

1 Explain the ferocity of the attack on Rathenau in 2.1.

2 Use the material in 2.2 to explain the exclusion of Jews from the Nazi Party.

3 How useful are 2.1, 2.2 and 2.3 to historians when trying to explain Hitler's electoral strategy between 1920 and 1929?

4 In what sense can the comments made by Goebbels in 2.4 be described as surprising?

5 What light does 2.5 throw on the circumstances in which Hitler was able to achieve power in January 1933?

Notes and references

1 Quoted in *Der Hitler Prozess* ('The Hitler trial'), the record of the court proceedings in Munich in 1924, Munich, 1913, pp. 262–69.

2 A. Hitler, *Mein Kampf*, Munich, 1925.

3 Hitler, *Mein Kampf*.

4 W. S. Allen, *The Nazi seizure of power*, New York, 1965, pp. 57–58.

5 J. Caplan, 'The rise of national socialism in modern Germany reconsidered', in G. Martel (ed.), *Modern Germany reconsidered*, London, 1992, p. 126.

3 The Nazi persecution of the Jews in Germany

Once in power, Hitler was able to indulge his extreme anti-Semitism openly. The first phase in his brutal attack on Germany's Jewish community would involve a legislative campaign which gradually deprived Jews of their civic rights. This campaign, which made a mockery of the legal process, would go hand in hand with a second objective, which was to persuade Jews to leave Germany altogether. Only when this second, emigration, option proved to be impractical would there be a move into the final phase of the manifestation of Nazi racial hatred: the mass murder of European and German Jews.

Hitler in power: the Jewish response

The response of the 525,000-strong Jewish community in Germany to the Nazi accession to power was initially one of calm. An editorial in a Jewish newspaper on 30 January 1933 noted that 'German Jews will not lose the calm they derive from their tie to all that is truly German'. The Jews hoped, despite the evidence to the contrary, that Nazism was merely a manifestation of restless, right-wing nationalism rather than of concentrated anti-Semitism. Once the Nazis were in power, the Jews argued, they would become less extreme when confronted by the responsibilities of government. Jewish leaders also comforted themselves with the knowledge that there were only three Nazis in the government appointed by von Hindenburg on 30 January 1933: Hitler, Hermann Göring and Wilhelm Frick. Jewish war veterans went to see Hans Lammers, the head of Hitler's Reich Chancellery on 4 April and presented him with a copy of a memorial book containing the names of the 12,000 Jewish soldiers who had died for Germany during the First World War. Hitler declined to see the veterans personally; it was, in fact, to be the last official contact between the government of the Third Reich and Jewish veterans' associations.

Despite increasingly sinister evidence about the Nazis' intentions regarding the Jews, a Jewish history professor was still able to announce in the summer of 1933 that he had voted for the Nazis since 1927. This was an extreme position, but some Jews were nevertheless reassured by the continuance in office of the aged President von Hindenburg, the personification of traditional, conservative, German values. It was also possible, others hoped, that the downward slide in the Nazi vote that had been evident in November 1932 would continue, and that the Nazis' time in power would be short. Jews whose families had lived in Germany for centuries allowed themselves, like other, non-Jewish, anti-Nazi,

Germans, to be lulled into a false sense of security. Indeed, in the immediate aftermath of Hitler's appointment as German chancellor the Nazis seemed to be more preoccupied with the communist, rather than the alleged Jewish, threat.

The shop boycott

The use of random thuggery by Nazi Brownshirts – as the brown-shirted members of the *Sturmabteilung* (SA), the Nazis' paramilitary arm, were called – had always been a feature of the Nazi movement. The 'brown trash', as their enemies called them, were always ready to pick on Jews – as well as communists – in the streets of Berlin and to beat them up.

On 1 April 1933 the SA was allowed to organise a boycott of Jewish shops all over Germany, but in the Nazis' eyes the results were disappointing. Ordinary Germans were either apathetic to the boycott or actually sympathetic to the plight of the Jews; some ostentatiously insisted on buying goods from Jewish shops as usual, despite the efforts of the SA louts to persuade them otherwise.

Hitler was directly involved in the shop boycott, telling cabinet members on 29 March that he had called for it; it would be a healthy way, he said, of releasing the anti-Semitic feelings of Nazi supporters. When foreigners complained (and there was a good deal of adverse foreign-press comment about the boycott, especially in the USA), this was the excuse that they were given: the boycott, the Nazis said, was a spontaneous demonstration of 'justifiable' anti-Jewish feeling. As a 'spontaneous' demonstration it was, in fact, a conspicuous failure. The Nazi newspaper, the *Völkischer Beobachter* ('National Observer') reported on 3 April that in the city of Hamburg (a centre of communist and socialist strength before 1933) some shoppers had even tried to force their way into a Jewish-owned shop. It seemed that German citizens had not all yet been brainwashed into accepting anti-Semitism.

Beneath the surface, however, was a rising current of vicious persecution of the Jews throughout Germany. While it was true that the first concentration camp, at Dachau, was built in 1933 to imprison communists and social democrats, eastern European Jews were among the first to be sent off to concentration camps. The historian Saul Friedländer[1] has pointed out that in the state of Hesse the SA broke into Jewish homes with the approval of local German inhabitants. Furthermore, individual Jews were murdered by the SA while the police did nothing. The rule of law had effectively ceased to operate from 30 January 1933 and the Jews were left with no legal protection.

The legal assault

If the majority of the German people took some time to be converted to the 'merits' of anti-Semitism, the Nazis were still able to use the law to exclude Jews from mainstream German life. Indeed, the process began by excluding Jews from membership of the legal profession itself: in March 1933 Jewish judges were instructed to retire from the bench and Jews were prevented from serving on juries.

President von Hindenburg was alarmed by the prospect of Jewish war veterans being discriminated against (although his concern for the Jews ended there). Three days after von Hindenburg had written to Hitler about the matter the Nazis introduced the Law for the Restoration of the Professional Standard of the Civil Service of April 1933. This law contained a clause exempting Jewish war veterans from its provisions (which was subsequently revoked) but stated that other Jews were now to be excluded from the German Civil Service. This was effected by the inclusion in the law of the so-called 'Aryan paragraph', which defined German citizens; Jews, as 'non-Aryans', were deemed 'racially unacceptable' and therefore could not be employed by the German state. The fourth point of the 1920 NSDAP programme (see Chapter 2) was now enshrined in German law, as a result of the help of bureaucratic time-servers who were only too happy to co-operate with the Nazis.

The pace of the Nazi legal assault on the Jews now increased. There was no political opposition to stop it, as by the summer of 1933 the Communist Party had been banned and the Social Democratic Party dissolved, while the Catholic Centre Party had obligingly disbanded itself. Hitler also banned free trade unions on 2 May 1933 (the day after he had decreed that May Day would be a public holiday).

In April 1933 Jewish children had a quota imposed upon them, whereby only 5 per cent of school places were allocated to them. Jewish academics were forced out of university posts and Jewish lawyers prevented from practising. Joseph Goebbels, Hitler's propaganda minister, established a Reich Chamber of Culture in September 1933 which excluded Jews from employment in the theatre, the film industry and the music profession. An 'Aryan paragraph' in the National Press Law prevented Jews from getting work as journalists; and so it went on.

The Nazis called their process of destroying democracy and free speech *Gleichschaltung* ('co-ordination' or 'bringing into line'), whereby every sector of German life was to be Nazified. Henceforward, making verbal complaints against anti-Semitism would become a criminal offence and the Jews would be at the mercy of a state machine that was motivated by the crudest form of racism.

The emigration option

Even more desirable for the Nazis than the exclusion of the Jews from the professions was their exclusion from Germany altogether. The Nazis therefore very quickly began to look for alternative territories where the German Jews could live.

An obvious place was Palestine, where a Jewish homeland had been established as a result of the 1917 Balfour Declaration, when the British foreign secretary, Arthur Balfour, had made a declaration saying that Jews would be allowed to settle in Palestine; there was no reference to the establishment of a Jewish state as such, however. A Jewish state was the ultimate aim of Jews like

Chaim Weizmann (1874–1952), a leading figure in the Zionist movement which wanted to establish such a state in the historical home of the Jewish people.

In 1917 Palestine had been part of the old Ottoman (Turkish) Empire, and at the end of the First World War the defeated Turkey lost its possessions in the Middle East. Britain obtained Palestine under a League of Nations mandate in 1920, which gave it control of the area until Palestine was deemed to be ready for self-government. The problem was that in making such a promise regarding a Jewish homeland to the Jews the British had offended the local Arab population and had therefore created regional tensions. Thousands of Jews, however, had already emigrated to Palestine, or Israel, as they called it, during the years after the First World War.

The Nazis were quite prepared to make a deal with the Jewish Agency for Palestine (the organisation which represented the Jews in Palestine) if this would rid them of German Jews by enabling them to be resettled in Palestine.

The 'Haavara Agreements'

In August 1933 the Jewish Agency for Palestine, which sponsored Jewish immigration to the region, concluded a series of agreements with the German Economics Ministry. Under the terms of these so-called 'Haavara Agreements', if German Jews left for Palestine they would pay money into a Jewish trust company. Once in Palestine, the immigrant would get half of the money back, in Palestine pounds; the other half would be used by the Jewish Agency to buy German goods, thus benefiting the German economy. Normally, Jews who emigrated from Nazi Germany could not take their savings with them, but in the interests of financial gain, and of ridding themselves of German Jews, the Nazis were prepared to bend the rules.

In this instance, Hitler proved that he could be pragmatic in order to act in Germany's economic interest. He even had the effrontery to claim that although Britain, the colonial power in Palestine, was trying to keep Jews out of Palestine (which was, in fact, partly true, as Britain did not want Jewish immigration to become out of control), Germany was helping them to go there. Those Jews who emigrated from Germany to Palestine during the 1930s proved to be the lucky ones.

The Madagascar Plan

Another Nazi scheme for the disposal of German Jews was the Madagascar Plan, which was discussed in Nazi leadership circles between 1938 and 1940. The idea was to create a sort of Jewish 'reservation' on the French colonial island of Madagascar, off the eastern coast of Africa. Heinrich Himmler, the Nazi police chief, seemed to favour the idea, writing to Hitler in May 1940 about the advantages of such a scheme, saying that he hoped 'to see the concept of Jews completely obliterated with the possibility of a large migration of all the Jews to Africa or else in a colony'.[2]

The problem with the Madagascar option was the island's geographical location: in the event of war, the British domination of the seas could render such a plan inoperative. Hitler and Himmler could also not have been certain that Germany would defeat France in the military campaign of 1940, and Madagascar was, after all, a French colony. Would the co-operation of the French have been forthcoming for such a scheme? Himmler and his aides do not seem to have been concerned about such problems. Nevertheless, the consideration of such plans to expel the Jews from Germany went hand in hand with the legal assault on their status inside the Reich.

The Nuremberg Laws

This legal assault on the Jews reached its peak with the laws adopted at the time of the 1935 Nazi Party rally at Nuremberg. Perhaps oddly, the Nuremberg Laws were passed at a time when some concern was being evinced in government circles about anti-Semitic excesses in Germany. In August 1935, for example, the finance minister, Hjalmar Schacht, complained about 'irresponsible Jew baiting', while the interior minister, Wilhelm Frick, even drafted an order to the state governments telling them to direct the police to intervene against illegal activity against Jews. The order was, in fact, never sent, as the Nazis feared that it would be regarded as a moderation of their anti-Jewish campaign. Nevertheless, the fact that Schacht had been able to make such a statement, and also went unpunished for it, is significant. The Nazi determination to exclude Jews from mainstream German life remained unaffected, however.

Lucy Dawidowicz has written that the Nuremberg Laws 'completed the disenfranchisement of the Jews of Germany'.[3] They made 'racial purity' a legal requirement for everyday German life and banned marriages between 'Aryans' and 'non-Aryans'. Jews were no longer able to vote in German elections, and a Reich Citizenship Law deprived them of their German citizenship. Thus German Jews, whose families may have lived in Germany for centuries, effectively became stateless people in their own country.

Hitler's racial and sexual obsessions were an obvious influence on the Nuremberg Laws. Jews were said to be 'alien' and were therefore forbidden to display the German flag. Similarly, only the 'racially pure' could be full German citizens, hence the withdrawal of the right of Jews to vote. Only those of German blood would be given a certificate of citizenship, so Jews were no longer 'citizens', but only 'subjects', of the Third Reich. Because, in Hitler's view, Jews might 'pollute' the 'German race', extra-marital relations between 'Aryans' and 'non-Aryans' were forbidden; neither could Jews employ a female German servant under 45 years of age (to avoid the perceived danger that Jewish men might seduce younger German women of child-bearing age and father children).

There were complicated provisions in the Nuremberg Laws to define who was, and who was not, a Jew. Three categories were legally defined:

1 'Jew';
2 'Mischling (part-Jew), first degree'; and
3 'Mischling, second degree'.

A 'Jew' was defined as someone with three fully Jewish grandparents; so, too, was someone who had two Jewish grandparents, belonged to a Jewish religious community, or joined one later, or who had married a Jew, either then or later. Anyone who was only one-eighth or one-sixteenth Jewish (that is, who had one Jewish great-grandparent or great-great-grandparent) would be considered German for legal purposes. The Nazis carried their programme of racial categorisation even further: as well as 'Jews' there were 'part-Jews' (*Mischlinge*). Someone who had two Jewish grandparents, who was not married to a Jew or was not a member of the local synagogue, was categorised as a '*Mischling*, first degree'. Those who had only one Jewish grandparent were defined as '*Mischlinge*, second degree'. A difference in a person's categorisation might ultimately have meant the difference between life and death.

The Jews had been banned from normal membership of German society by the Nuremberg Laws. The process was completed by a further decree, in late December 1935, whereby Jewish professors, teachers and doctors who were still employed because they had obtained an exemption from earlier laws were dismissed.

The impact of the Nuremberg Laws

According to Nazi statistics for the year 1935, there were 750,000 Germans who could be categorised as 'part-Jews' of the first and second degree. There were 475,000 'full Jews' who practised their religion (that is, they attended a synagogue regularly) and a further 300,000 'full Jews' who did not. This made a grand total of over 1½ million people with a degree of Jewish blood, or 2.3 per cent of the entire German population in 1935.

Other minorities

It is important to note that other groups of people were discriminated against by the Law for the Protection of German Blood and German Honour, which was part of the Nuremberg Laws. This stated, on 15 September 1935, that Germans could not marry or have sexual relations with people of 'alien blood'. Days later, the Ministry of the Interior defined such persons as 'Gypsies, negroes and their bastards'.

Exceptions to the Nuremberg Laws

The Nazis could be pragmatic when it suited them, and made some exceptions to the Nuremberg Laws. A well-known case, highlighted by Saul Friedländer,[4] was that of General Erhard Milch, a leading air-force officer who subsequently became the organisation's inspector general. He was a *Mischling* of the second degree who was recategorised as an 'Aryan' (it is likely that Hitler himself made the decision in this case). Rumours also circulated about the Jewish origins of Himmler's deputy, Reinhard Heydrich; in his case, the relevant documents mysteriously disappeared.

The irony is that neither Hitler nor many other leading Nazis were 'true Germans' because they had not been brought up in Germany. Hitler was an

Austrian; Rudolf Hess, Hitler's deputy until 1941, was brought up in Egypt; the Nazi propagandist Alfred Rosenberg came from Estonia; Walther Darré, the minister of food and agriculture, had been educated in part in England; while the leader of the Hitler Youth, Baldur von Schirach, could have qualified as a US citizen because his mother was American. These men, among others, representing a ragbag of ethnic influences, masterminded the racial uniformity demanded in Nazi Germany.

The Austrian model

While they were eager to destroy the rights of Jews within the Third Reich, the Nazis continued to pursue their efforts to exclude Jews from Germany altogether. In March 1938 Germany occupied Austria and thus achieved Hitler's long-held ambition for an *Anschluss* ('union') between his homeland and Germany. Austria had a sizeable Jewish population and would provide a model for the Nazis' attempts to 'persuade' Jews to leave Germany (exactly how this was achieved is discussed in Chapter 4.)

The immediate result of the *Anschluss* was a vicious Jew-baiting campaign. The centre of this campaign was Vienna, the Austrian capital, which had a large Jewish population. Older Jews were forced by the SA to clean pavements with small brushes in the sight of jeering Viennese spectators; others were beaten up and their homes looted by Austrian Nazi thugs; Jewish businesses were

Jews forced to scrub the streets of Vienna watched by a jeering crowd in 1938.

expropriated, too. Known criminals were encouraged by the Nazis to terrorise and intimidate the 190,000 Austrian Jews. The situation became so out of control, however, that on 17 March Heydrich was forced to threaten with arrest 'those National Socialists who in the last few days allowed themselves to launch large-scale assaults in a totally undisciplined way' against Jews (even then, the indiscriminate violence directed against Jews took some days to die down). The events in Austria would prefigure what would happen in Germany itself later in 1938.

After the Second World War Austrians preferred to present themselves as 'victims' of the Third Reich, but this was, at best, only partially true. Hitler himself was an Austrian, as were some of the worst SS (*Schutzstaffel* – the Nazi 'protection echelon') killers, like Adolf Eichmann. The ferocity of Austrian anti-Semitism in 1938 had its origins in the hatred and resentment of Jews stirred up by propagandists like Karl Lueger and August von Schönerer before the First World War. Although the Austrian social democrats stood for democracy, the forces of the political right in inter-war Austria were undemocratic and racist in their orientation. The anti-Semitic events of 1938, following the triumph of the extreme right, can therefore be said to have been predictable. One historian has written of anti-Semitism that 'Nowhere was it more striking than in Austria in March 1938, where it welled up spontaneously during the euphoria accompanying its annexation by Germany.'[5] The hysterical welcome given to Hitler when he returned to Vienna in triumph in 1938 showed that anti-Semitism was a popular policy with most Austrians. The fanatical anti-Semitism of the failed artist who had left Vienna in 1913 could now be given full vent in his homeland.

One Jew's experience

While it is always hard to comprehend the vicious nature of the racism imposed by the Nazis, people's testimonies can give valuable insights into how such persecution affected individuals and their families.

Such an experience has been movingly chronicled in the diaries of Victor Klemperer.[6] Klemperer was a German Jew who had converted to Christianity (which proved no safeguard for those who were racially defined as 'Jews'). He was a professor in Dresden who hoped, like others, that after the early anti-Semitic excesses of Nazism the worst would be over. Klemperer, along with many other German Jews, regarded Germany as his country and opted to stay there although he had the chance to leave. In his diaries, he chronicled in depressing detail how Nazi racism impinged on every aspect of Jewish life: for example, he noticed that even a tube of toothpaste in a local chemist's shop had a swastika on it.

Some manifestations of Nazi racism were clearly absurd: for instance, all Jews, Klemperer noted, were obliged to write in Hebrew, even when they only knew the German language, while orthodox Jews (who followed strict dietary codes) were forced to get their supplies of meat from Denmark. Perhaps even worse was the social ostracism of the Jews that was imposed by the Nazis, and Klemperer was ignored by his former friends at work. He ultimately came to write in his diary 'Whoever is not a mortal enemy of Nazism is not my friend.' By the time he wrote these words, however, it was too late to escape, and Klemperer, like so many other German Jews, perished during the Nazi persecution.

Those Jews who remained in Germany did so because they could not believe that such a racist system could prevail in a supposedly civilised European country in the twentieth century. The irony was that before 1933 German Jews were more fully integrated into mainstream society (despite the prejudice against them from the political right) than their counterparts in Britain and France.

Document case study

The Nazi persecution of the Jews

3.1 The Jewish response, 1933

I am afraid that we are merely at the beginning of a process aiming, purposefully and according to a well-prepared plan, at the economic and moral annihilation of all members, without any distinctions, of the Jewish race living in Germany.

Source: Georg Solmssen, a Jewish financier, quoted in S. Friedländer, *Nazi Germany and the Jews*, London, 1997, p.33

3.2 The shop boycott, 1933

The action committees must at once popularise the boycott by means of propaganda and enlightenment. The principle is: No German must any longer buy from a Jew or let him and his backers promote their goods. The boycott must be general. It must be supported by the whole German people and must hit Jewry where it is most vulnerable.

Source: part of an order issued by the *Gauleiter* (regional Nazi leaders), 1933, quoted in L. Dawidowicz, *The war against the Jews, 1933–45*, London, 1975, p. 99

3.3 The Nuremberg Laws, 1935

Law for the Protection of German Blood and German Honour, 15 September 1935.

Entirely convinced that the purity of German blood is essential to the further existence of the German people, and inspired by the uncompromising determination to safeguard the future of the German nation, the Reichstag has unanimously adopted the following law, which is promulgated herewith:

1 Marriages between Jews and citizens of German or kindred blood are forbidden . . .
2 Sexual relations between Jews and nationals of German or kindred blood are forbidden.

Source: extract from the Nuremberg Laws, 1935

3.4 Jewish survival under persecution

I believe ever more strongly that Hitler really does embody the soul of the German people, that he really stands for 'Germany' and that he will consequently maintain himself and justifiably maintain himself. Whereby I have not only outwardly lost my fatherland. And even if the government should change one day: my inner sense of belonging is gone.

Source: Victor Klemperer, 17 August 1938, *I shall bear witness. The diaries of Victor Klemperer, 1933–41*, London, 1998

3.5 A Jew who escaped

If my grandfather had been paid fairly for his business, he would have been able to get the rest of the family out of Germany. But he was not. He and my grandmother arrived in New York in 1939 with 10 marks – $2.50 in US money – in their pockets.

Source: Catherine Noren, 'We escaped from Hitler's Germany', in R. K. Chartock and J. Spencer (eds.), *Can it happen again? Chronicles of the Holocaust*, New York, 1995, p. 59

Document case-study questions

1 To what extent was there a 'well-prepared plan' for dealing with the 'Jewish question' when the Nazis came to power, according to 3.1?

2 From your reading of 3.2, what principle underlaid the 1933 shop boycott and how effectively was it applied?

3 How valuable a source is 3.3 for a historian of the Nazi period?

4 What do we learn from the tone of 3.4 about the attitude of Jews to the Nazi regime by the late 1930s?

5 What link can you establish between the feelings shown in 3.4 and 3.5?

Notes and references

1 S. Friedländer, *Nazi Germany and the Jews*, London, 1997, p. 18.

2 L. Dawidowicz, *The war against the Jews, 1933–45*, London, 1975, p. 156.

3 Dawidowicz, *War against the Jews*, p. 101.

4 Friedländer, *Germany and the Jews*, p. 153.

5 D. Goldhagen, *Hitler's willing executioners. Ordinary Germans and the Holocaust*, London, 1996, p. 286.

6 V. Klemperer, *I shall bear witness. The diaries of Victor Klemperer, 1933–41*, London, 1998.

4 The coming of the Holocaust, 1938–41

Three issues will be discussed in this chapter.

1 Was the Holocaust the result of a long-term plan or intention on Hitler's part to exterminate the Jews? (Historians who accept this view have become known as 'intentionalists' and argue that such a blueprint can be found in Hitler's book, *Mein Kampf*, which was written during the 1920s, and in speeches that Hitler made after he came to power in 1933.)
2 Alternatively, was the Holocaust the result of a short-term, wartime emergency? (By 1942 enormous numbers of eastern European Jews had fallen under Nazi control, and it has been suggested by some historians that the Holocaust, or 'Final Solution', as the Nazis euphemistically called it, was a response to this situation. There were too many Jews in the eastern ghettos and the Nazis believed that they would have to be liquidated. Those so-called 'structuralist' or 'functionalist' historians who accept this explanation also argue that Hitler had no long-term plan to murder the Jews *en masse*, and therefore played no central role in the 'Final Solution'.)
3 At what point was the decision to start implementing the 'Final Solution' made? (This issue is important because it may have been linked to Hitler's decision to invade the Soviet Union in June 1941.)

Kristallnacht

In order to answer the above questions, it is necessary to be aware of the course of events, and, in particular, to understand the major turning points which led to the genesis of the Holocaust between 1938 and 1941. Chapter 3 outlined the history of the Nazi legislative persecution of the Jews after Hitler came to power in 1933. Before 1938, however, incidences of violence against Jews were on a relatively small scale, and were carried out in a fairly random fashion by the brown-shirted thugs of the SA, whom critics of Nazism referred to as the 'brown trash'.

All this changed on the night of 9–10 November 1938 – *Kristallnacht* ('crystal night', named after the crystal-like shards of broken glass from the shattered windows of Jewish properties). It began with an act of personal revenge by a Jew and ended in a state-sponsored orgy of violence against Jews and their property throughout Germany.

The act of personal revenge took place in Paris, France, on 7 November 1938, when Herschel Grynszpan, a 17-year-old Jew, shot and fatally wounded Ernst vom Rath, a diplomat at the German Embassy (ironically, vom Rath was under surveillance by the Nazi secret police, the Gestapo (*Geheime Staatspolizei*), at the time, as a suspected member of the anti-Hitler resistance movement in Germany). Grynszpan's act was a direct response to the German government's action in dumping 17,000 Jews along the Polish–German frontier in appalling conditions, in order to prevent the Poles from enforcing a ban on the re-entry of Polish Jews from Germany into Poland. Two of these Jews were Grynszpan's parents.

Vom Rath died of his wounds on 9 November, upon news of which SA men and NSDAP members attacked and burned down Jewish synagogues throughout Germany; Jewish homes and businesses were also destroyed, while physical assaults were made on Jewish men, women and children. In all, 191 synagogues were burned down and 36 Jews killed in Berlin alone. Across Germany, the death toll rose to 91, with 7,500 businesses being destroyed. Perhaps even more disturbing was the arrest and imprisonment of 30,000 Jewish men in concentration camps at Dachau, Buchenwald and Sachsenhausen. A major turning point in the Nazi policy towards the Jews seemed to have been reached.

The responsibility for *Kristallnacht*

The Nazis attempted to portray *Kristallnacht* as a popular, spontaneous reaction of outrage on the news of vom Rath's death. It was nothing of the sort, however.

Intentionalist historians, like Lucy Dawidowicz, have emphasised the fact that Hitler himself said nothing publicly, either about vom Rath's assassination or the anti-Jewish violence that it allegedly provoked. In fact, the villain of the piece seems to have been Joseph Goebbels, the propaganda minister, who was motivated, according to the SS chief, Heinrich Himmler, a long-time rival, by lust for power. But we need not doubt that Goebbels' inflammatory speech in Munich on 9 November, which inspired the attacks on Jewish lives and properties, had Hitler's tacit approval. It may well have suited the *Führer* to encourage the rivalry between such powerful Nazi leaders as Goebbels, Himmler and Himmler's deputy, Reinhard Heydrich, because all were perceived by Hitler to be radical on the 'Jewish question'. Ultimately, all can be said to have benefited from *Kristallnacht*, which was estimated to have destroyed half the amount of plate glass produced annually in Belgium (the country from which the Germans usually imported their plate glass). Hermann Göring, the organiser of Hitler's Four-year Plan for the economy (which started in 1936 and was designed to make Germany self-sufficient), also pretended to deplore the destruction of *Kristallnacht*, saying that 'they don't harm the Jew but me, who is the final authority for co-ordinating the German economy'. Yet Göring was about to take the initiative in the acceleration of the plan to eliminate the 'Jew from the Germany economy'.

The aftermath of *Kristallnacht*

Göring did so at a general meeting of Nazi leaders that he convened on 12 November 1938. In theory, German insurance companies should have covered the cost of the destroyed Jewish businesses, and it was agreed at the

Adolf Hitler with Heinrich Himmler in 1938. As head of the SS, Himmler was responsible more than any other Nazi for the planning and implementation of the policy to exterminate the Jewish people in Europe.

meeting that if the German insurers were to retain their credibility they had to pay for the damage. Göring, however, made a mockery of this commitment by suggesting a counter-proposal: the German government would allow the payments to be made, but would then confiscate the money from the Jews, so making them liable for the repair of their damaged buildings.

On the same day, 12 November 1938 – a crucial date in the campaign against German Jewry – Göring also issued the Decree on the Penalty Payment by Jews who are German Subjects, which required the Jewish community to pay 1 billion Reichmarks in a fine imposed because of the Jews' 'hostile attitude . . . towards the German *Volk* and Reich'. A further decree made on that day, entitled the Decree on Eliminating the Jew from German Economic Life, excluded Jews from the retail trade, the management of German companies, the selling of any goods or services and employment as independent craftsmen; in short, from any type of participation in the economic life of Germany.

Further measures taken in the month of November 1938, in which Goebbels and Heydrich both played leading roles, banned Jewish children from attending state schools and allowed local-government authorities to impose curfew restrictions on Jews. In the following month, the request made by Goebbels at the meeting of 12 November, that Jews should be banned from public places, like theatres, cinemas and beaches, was agreed to by Hitler. The momentum of the anti-Jewish campaign therefore increased demonstrably in the aftermath of *Kristallnacht*.

The historical debate

Intentionalist historians, like Lucy Dawidowicz, who believe in the concept of a blueprint for the 'Final Solution' dating back to the 1920s, see *Kristallnacht* as an important turning point in the Nazis' anti-Semitic policy. Dawidowicz argues that the pogrom (the word now commonly used to describe an anti-Jewish outrage) 'provided the National Socialist government with the opportunity, short of actual war, to proceed with the total expropriation of the Jews and the complete removal of their freedom'.[1]

By contrast, structuralist historians, like Martin Broszat and Hans Mommsen, continue to deny that there was a set plan behind the Nazis' anti-Jewish policy before 1941. Mommsen famously called Hitler a 'weak dictator', who was surrounded by powerful Nazis, such as Goebbels, Himmler and Göring, who wanted to increase their own power and influence. If we accept this polycratic model (meaning a system in which there are rival power centres), then *Kristallnacht* is a manifestation of the Nazis' internal power struggle in the Third Reich, in which Hitler becomes a less significant figure. The structuralists deny that Hitler, whom they regard as being a weak and muddle-headed leader, had either the power or the clarity of vision to evolve a long-term plan for the destruction of the Jews.

It is important to note, however, that contemporary historians do not argue in such stark terms as Dawidowicz, Mommsen and Broszat did during the 1970s.

Historians like Ian Kershaw support a synthesis of both positions, acknowledging the central importance of Hitler's position but also seeing the wartime situation as being crucial in the evolution of the Holocaust. ②

In this often complex historical debate the evidence can often seem confusing. As indicated earlier in this chapter, Dawidowicz can find no record of a public statement made by Hitler on *Kristallnacht*, yet a Propaganda Ministry official reported that when Goebbels told Hitler about his plans for a pogrom the *Führer* 'squealed with delight and slapped his thigh in his enthusiasm', implying that the pogrom had his full approval. Can it be assumed, as the structuralists do, that the lack of Hitler's proven imprint on an event like *Kristallnacht* means that he was not fully involved in the decision-making for it? (It was, after all, Göring who said 'In the last analysis, it is the *Führer* alone who decides'.) The issue of Hitler's role in the escalation of the Nazi anti-Jewish policies of terror and genocide is therefore a central one in the debate about the 'Final Solution' and will be returned to later in this chapter.

The emigration option

By the end of 1938 the Jews had effectively been driven out of everyday German life. The so-called 'Jewish question' remained for the Nazis, however, as Heydrich noted at the 12 November 1938 meeting, namely to kick the Jew out of Germany. Heydrich, the head of the RSHA (*Reichssicherheitshauptamt*, the Reich Security Head Office), suggested that the forced emigration of Jews, as had been briefly used in the episode that provoked vom Rath's assassination, should be tried. He suggested that if Jews would not leave Germany voluntarily as a result of the systematic discrimination against, and persecution of, them, as practised by the Nazi government since 1933, then they must be forced to go.

Heydrich, who would assume an increasingly prominent role in the evolution of anti-Jewish policy in the Nazi regime, pointed to the experience of the authorities in Austria, which had been forcibly integrated into the German Reich by means of the *Anschluss* in March 1938. There, the SS leader Adolf Eichmann had been involved in anti-Jewish terror in the immediate aftermath of the *Anschluss*, with apparently 'satisfactory' results. Between March and September 1938 45,000 Austrian Jews had been 'persuaded' to leave their homeland, and another 100,000 would do so before the outbreak of the Second World War in September 1939. The emigration of Austrian Jews had, of course, been achieved as a result of a great deal of intimidation and thuggery (nowhere in the pre-war Third Reich was anti-Semitism more virulent than in Vienna), but Heydrich also admired the bureaucratic apparatus that Eichmann had devised with which to deal with the Jews. Firstly, Eichmann had set up a Central Office for Jewish Emigration and, secondly, he had re-established the old Jewish Religious Community and through it worked with Jewish leaders who had been released from camps or prison. Why some Jewish community leaders felt able to co-operate with the Nazis in this way has become a controversial historical issue. Many historians argue that, trapped as they were in an impossible situation, they felt that they had little choice. For his part, Eichmann used their influence to persuade their fellow Jews to leave Austria, but there seems little doubt that these leaders were terrorised into co-operation.

Eichmann's experiment in Austria provided a model for the rest of the Third Reich as well, and in January 1939 Heydrich received authorisation from Göring to establish the Reich Central Office for Jewish Emigration. The question facing Heydrich was where these emigrating Jews were supposed to go. The Western democracies certainly showed little enthusiasm for accepting a mass influx of Jews, who, rather than 'emigrating' from their native Germany, where Jews had lived for centuries, were effectively being expelled.

The Nazis came up with some ingenious answers to Heydrich's problem, as follows (although in the event they would all be rendered inoperative by the coming of war in 1939):

1 Palestine;
2 Madagascar; and
3 Poland.

Palestine

As far back as 1933 the Nazis had made the 'Haavara Agreements' with the Jewish Agency in Palestine, then a British mandate under the League of Nations, to allow German Jews to emigrate there. However, now non-German Jews were under German control following the Third Reich's annexation of Austria, as well as the Czech Sudetenland later in 1938.

Madagascar

In November 1938 Hitler had spoken to Göring about the possibility of sending Jews from Germany to the island of Madagascar, off the eastern coast of Africa. On the face of it this was a bizarre suggestion, as Madagascar was then under French colonial rule (although US President F. D. Roosevelt had also supported the idea of sending Jews to Portuguese Angola), but it was in line with comments made by Hitler to the South African defence minister to the effect that 'some day, the Jews will disappear from Europe'. In the short term, the Madagascar Plan was put on hold until Germany's defeat of France in the summer of 1940. It was then resurrected (see document 4.1), but remained dependent on two things: firstly, the goodwill of Britain, and, secondly, a proposed peace settlement between Germany and Britain in 1940, which was ultimately never concluded. Nevertheless, as historians of the Holocaust have pointed out, the Nazis' interest in Madagascar appears to show that Hitler, along with other Nazi leaders, like Himmler, took the Madagascar Plan seriously between 1938 and 1940. This can be seen as evidence of Hitler's desire to devolve the 'Jewish question' to other countries.

Poland

The expulsion of Polish Jews into a 'no-man's land' on the German–Polish frontier in 1938, before *Kristallnacht*, has already been discussed earlier in this chapter. Poland remained a focus of Nazi interest as a possible site for a Jewish 'reservation'. Thus in October 1939 Eichmann received orders to deport a number of Jews living in the Nazi protectorate of Bohemia–Moravia (formerly Czecho-slovakian territory, which had been occupied by the Germans in March 1939) and in Upper Silesia (formerly Polish territory, which had been acquired by Germany after its victory over Poland in September 1939). A potential 'reservation' site had been found at Nisko, on the river San, near the Polish city of Lublin, before the operation was abruptly cancelled by orders from Berlin, leaving the Jews to find their own way back to their original points of departure. This abrupt change of policy was apparently caused by the arrival in German-occupied territory in Poland of large numbers of Germans from Soviet-held territory in Poland following the partition of Poland as agreed by the Nazi–Soviet Pact of August 1939. For the Nazis, the welfare of ethnic Germans obviously took priority over dealing with the Jews.

The Nazi hierarchy thus wrestled with the question of what to do with 'unwanted' Jews, a problem which became more urgent after the German military victories in Poland and the USSR between 1939 and 1941. A suggestion by Göring that rich US and Canadian Jews should be persuaded to buy land for Jewish resettlement in North America had, perhaps predictably, proved to be impractical. Between November 1938 and the late summer of 1941 the emigration (or, in reality, the expulsion) of Jews seems to have been the preferred option of Hitler and his colleagues.

Hitler's speech of 30 January 1939

While his subordinates pondered on what to do so with the Third Reich's Jewish population early in 1939, Hitler made one of his great, set-piece speeches in the Reichstag, whose importance has been differently assessed by intentionalist and structuralist historians.

Days before, Hitler had told the Czech foreign minister, 'We are going to destroy the Jews. They are not going to get away with what they did on 9 November 1918.' This reiterated an important theme in Hitler's personal anti-Semitism (discussed in Chapter 1). Like many Germans, Hitler believed that the 'Fatherland' had been betrayed by Jews and Bolsheviks in 1918 and that this was why Germany had lost the First World War. He was determined not to allow it to happen again.

Hitler returned to this theme in his speech of 30 January 1939, warning that 'If international-finance Jewry within Europe and abroad should succeed once more in plunging the peoples into a world war' this would result in the 'destruction of the Jewish race in Europe'.[2] Regardless of whether Germany was victorious in the world war that Hitler referred to or not, the fate of the Jews, it seemed, was sealed. This, at least, is how intentionalists, like Lucy Dawidowicz, interpret the speech. But Hitler, as the historian Michael Marrus points out, had made apparently 'unalterable' decisions before and had then changed them. One of the most famous examples of his changes of mind occurred in 1938, shortly before the Munich Conference, when Hitler said that he would 'destroy Czechoslovakia' by force; yet two months later Hitler accepted a partial solution which weakened, but did not destroy, the Czech state by detaching the majority-German-speaking area of the Sudetenland from it. Marrus underlines the importance of noting the difference between what Hitler said and what Hitler did. Nonetheless, there is still good reason for accepting Hitler's threat: that if Hitler's Germany were to be defeated in a world war he would take the Jews down with him in an orgy of destruction (which, after all, is what he actually did). A German victory, however, might have allowed a more leisurely solution to the 'Jewish question' by means of the mass expulsion of Jews – this, at least, is what the structuralists seem to imply. This minor case study highlights the essential difficulty involved in the study of the Holocaust: how seriously can we take Hitler's rhetoric from the time when *Mein Kampf* was written onwards?

The decision for genocide

Because the failure to reach any terms with Britain in the summer of 1940 ruled out the Madagascar Plan, and because Nazi regional leaders disliked the 'ghetto solution' (that is, herding Jews into specific areas of Polish cities, like Warsaw and Lodz), the Nazis had to consider other options with which to solve the 'Jewish question'. The Nazi leaders were not concerned about the appalling conditions in the ghettos, but the *Gauleiter* (Nazi regional leaders) in occupied Poland complained bitterly about the number of Jews who were being forced into these constricted areas. At some point during 1941 the 'advantages' of a programme of mass killings of Jews was therefore beginning to be favoured by the Nazis over the concept of a mass expulsion of Jews from Europe. The SS chief, Himmler, was aware that the technology for mass gassings was available: it had already been tried in Germany, in the so-called 'Operation Euthanasia', whereby 70,000 chronically sick and disabled hospital patients had been deliberately murdered. Operation Euthanasia was implemented in early 1941, but gassing would not be used against the Jews until later in the year.

At what point was the decision to murder the European Jews *en masse* taken? Again, historians have debated this issue. Dawidowicz, for example, argues that the crucial decision must have been taken between December 1940 and March 1941. She believes that Operation Barbarossa (the codename for the German invasion of the USSR, launched in June 1941) and the 'disorder of war would provide Hitler with the cover for unchecked commission of murder'; for her, 'war and the annihilation of the Jews were interdependent'.[3]

There are two problems with Dawidowicz's argument. First of all, the preparations for the systematic murder of the Jews did not begin until the autumn of 1941, some three months after Operation Barbarossa was launched. Secondly, as Marrus points out, the systematic gassing of Jews did not begin until March 1942, more than two years after the outbreak of war. Why, Marrus has asked, did the Nazis wait so long to murder Jews *en masse*, when Dawidowicz claims that war would provide the 'cover' for the Holocaust? During the early phases of the war in the USSR (and earlier, in Poland), the Nazis had favoured mass shootings – not just of Jews, but also of Poles, Russians and Gypsies (other groups of people whom the Nazis deemed 'racially inferior'). This work was allocated to the SS *Einsatzgruppen* ('task forces'), the special killing squads that followed behind the advancing German army in eastern Europe.

It is possible, in fact, that two decisions were made about the fate of European Jewry: one as early as March 1941, when a decision was made to eliminate Soviet Jews, and a second probably in September 1941, when a further decision was taken to murder all European Jews.

A war of revenge

For an intentionalist historian like Dawidowicz, such a division of decision-making is not that important, because in her view war provided Hitler with a cover for his long-stated intention to eliminate the Jews. Another leading intentionalist historian, Andreas Hillgruber, supports Dawidowicz's view that the invasion of the USSR can be linked with Hitler's long-standing intention to murder the Jews.

For structuralists like Broszat and Mommsen, however, the decision-making distinction is an important one. Their view is that somehow, under the pressures of war and as a result of German setbacks on the Eastern Front, the Nazi campaign against the Jews escalated, partly also in response to complaints by the *Gauleiter* that they had too many Jews under their jurisdiction. The 'Final Solution' in effect therefore became an act of revenge linked to Hitler's ideological war against Bolshevism on the Eastern Front. Hitler's loathing of communism, which he frequently associated with Judaism, was, after all, well known.

The problem with the structuralist theory (according to which the Nazis apparently somehow blundered into the 'Final Solution'), as the distinguished German historian Karl Dietrich Bracher has pointed out, is that in ignoring the issue of responsibility 'they have fallen into the danger of . . . underestimating and trivializing National Socialism'.[4]

This brings us inevitably back to the question of Hitler's responsibility for the Holocaust. At one extreme, there is the unsustainable view, put forward by the right-wing British historian David Irving during the 1970s, that because there is no document in existence ordering the 'Final Solution' that is signed by the *Führer* this is proof that Hitler did not know about it. This argument is debatable as Hitler often gave orders verbally, a technique which became known to his subordinates as 'it is the *Führer's* wish'.

At the other extreme is the question of what would have happened if Hitler had died in the summer of 1941, before the 'Final Solution' was under way. Regarding this question, a recent study by Philippe Burrin concludes that 'For things to escalate into a holocaust Hitler's impetus was needed, an impetus with deep roots.'[5]

Burrin occupies a middle position between the intentionalist and structuralist schools of the 1970s, and this is the one that is now normally adopted by historians. According to this view, Hitler's personal role in the Holocaust is fully acknowledged (even the structuralist Broszat recognises that Hitler was an evil leader), but so is that of others. The German army, for example, colluded in the round-up and murder of Jews in eastern Europe; the German churches remained largely silent about the fate of the Jews; thousands of middle-ranking German bureaucrats co-operated in the transportation of Jews to death camps; while there was what Burrin calls 'widespread moral indifference' in Germany to their fate.

After allowing for all the alternative explanations of how the Holocaust came about, however, the central role of Hitler in the 'Final Solution' remains crucial to an understanding of the process of genocide which began in 1941. It was Hitler's racism, much more than his anti-communism, which provided the essential impetus for the 'Final Solution'.

The road to the death camps

The long-standing and often complex historical debate about the 'Final Solution' can tend to switch the focus dangerously away from what actually happened to why it happened. Despite the historians' arguments about exactly when the decision to implement the 'Final Solution' was taken, certain crucial signposts on the road to genocide (involving the Germany army, as well as the SS) have been recognised by all historians.

One of these significant pointers was the order to the German army to use 'ruthless and energetic measures' against Jews and anti-German resisters in the USSR after the German invasion began, and especially against the political officers (commissars) of the Soviet Communist Party. This directive, which was issued by the German High Command on 6 June 1941, was followed by the infamous directive from Göring to Heydrich of 31 July 1941 (see document 4.2) ordering Heydrich to solve the 'Jewish question'.

Behind the German lines the *Einsatzgruppen* were finding the crude method of mass shootings an unsatisfactory one and, as always, Himmler was receptive to the 'sensitivities' of his men. By September 1941 *Einsatzgruppe* C was in possession of a truck which used exhaust gases to kill its victims, and Eichmann was recommending the use of carbon monoxide with which to gas people while they were taking showers. More efficient methods of killing were therefore available to the Nazis by the autumn of 1941. Nevertheless, it is important to note that hundreds of thousands of Jews were killed in so-called 'pit killings' (mass shootings) in eastern Europe before the 'stationary killings' in the death camps began.

With the technology decided upon, it remained only to find sites for the mass gassings and to construct *Vernichtungslager* ('annihilation camps'). The first death camp was built at Chelmno, in Poland, where the gassing of Jews began on 8 December 1941, using exhaust gases from vans. At around the same time, gas trucks were also used to kill Jews in Semlin, Serbia (the Germans had invaded Yugoslavia in March 1941) after the German army, to quote Dawidowicz, had

German troops shooting three victims in a forest in the east, 1941.

been 'embarrassingly efficient'⁶ in rounding up local Jews. The next death camp, at Belzec, again in Poland, was operational in February 1942, and the momentum of mass murder built up in that year with the opening of new death camps at Sobibor, Majdanek and Treblinka, all in Poland.

The Wannsee Conference

On 20 January 1942 Heydrich convened a conference at Wannsee, the Berlin suburb in which the RSHA headquarters was based. He was the only top-ranking Nazi to attend, but representatives of the Interior, Justice and Foreign Ministries were present, as were those from the occupied territories in the east, 13 in all.

Some historians have seen the Wannsee Conference as the final phase of the decision-making process which led to the 'Final Solution', but, as we have seen, the gassing of Jews predated the conference. Much time was spent at the conference in discussing the status of Jewish partners in mixed marriages, but the basic purpose of the conference seems to have been to co-ordinate the efforts of different sections of the Nazi government in the furtherance of their common aim – the mass murder of European Jewry (see document 4.3).

A more recent view, by Burrin, sees the Wannsee Conference as merely recording a 'solution reached in mid-October [1941] by Himmler and his men',⁷

Reinhard Heydrich, Himmler's subordinate who chaired the Wannsee Conference, was one of the foremost Nazis involved in devising the 'Final Solution'. Heydrich was assassinated in Prague by Czech freedom fighters in May 1942.

and certainly, by the time of the Wannsee meeting, the 'Final Solution' was well under way. In the view of another leading historian, Ian Kershaw, the Wannsee Conference was merely about the logistics of mass murder.

Conclusion

There is an ongoing debate amongst historians about the circumstances in which Hitler and other Nazi leaders made the decision to implement what they called the *Endlösung* ('Final Solution'). There is, however, a measure of agreement about the point at which the decision was made, for up to mid-September 1941 a territorial option, which favoured the expulsion of the Jews from Germany to some sort of massive 'reservation' in the east, was still a possible solution. The fact that the Germans had not won their expected overwhelming victory over the Soviet Red army after the three months of fighting since June 1941 clearly contributed to the decision to turn the deportation of Jews into their murder. As we have seen, the Nazi *Gauleiter* were also complaining that there were too many Jews in the occupied territories, while the SS was straining to find a solution to the 'Jewish question'. Finally, it was Hitler who ordered the deportation of German Jews to the east in September 1941 as a prelude to their gassing. As his colleague, Goebbels, recognised, Hitler was the 'unswerving protagonist and advocate of a radical solution'. It merely remained for the Nazis to solve the technical problems associated with the inhuman process of the 'Final Solution', a matter which Hitler was prepared to leave to his subordinates.

1938 *7 November:* vom Rath fatally wounded in Paris.

9–10 November: Kristallnacht.

12 November: Göring's meeting to co-ordinate measures against German Jews.

1939 *30 January:* Hitler's Reichstag speech threatening the Jews with extinction in the event of war.

1 September: Germany invades Poland.

1940 *22 June:* France surrenders to Germany.

1941 *6 June:* the German High Command issues the 'commissar' order.

22 June: Operation Barbarossa launched.

31 July: Göring's directive to Heydrich ordering him to solve the 'Jewish question'.

15 September (?): the probable date of Hitler's decision to implement the beginning of the 'Final Solution'.

8 December: the gassing of Jews starts at Chelmno.

1942 *20 January:* the Wannsee Conference.

Figure 2. A timeline of key events in German history, 1938–42.

Document case study

The Nazi plans for the mass expulsion of German Jewry

4.1 The Madagascar Plan

Another very important point is the decision of the *Führer*, which he made at my request, that there will be no more transports of Jews into the area of the Government-General. As a general political observation I would like to state that it is planned to transport the whole pack of Jews [*Judensippschaft*] from the German Reich, the Government-General and the Protectorate, in the shortest conceivable time after peace has been made, to an African or American Colony. Madagascar is being considered, to be ceded by France for this purpose. There will be ample room here for a few million Jews on an area of 500,000 sq. kms. I have tried to let the Jews in the Government-General also share in this advantage, of building up a new life on new land. This has been accepted so that there should be a tremendous easing within sight.

Source: from a speech by Hans Frank, the Nazi governor-general of occupied Poland, on the Madagascar Plan, 12 July 1940

4.2 Göring's 'Final Solution' directive

To the Chief of the Security Police and the SD,
SS *Gruppenführer* [Lieutenant General] Heydrich
Berlin

In completion of the task which was entrusted to you in the Edict dated January 24, 1939, of solving the Jewish question by means of emigration or evacuation in the most convenient way possible, given the present conditions, I herewith charge you with making all necessary preparation with regard to organisational, practical and financial aspects for an overall solution [*Gesamtlösung*] of the Jewish question in the German sphere of influence in Europe.

Insofar as the competencies of other central organisations are affected, these are to be involved.

I further charge you with submitting to me promptly an overall plan of the preliminary organisational, practical and financial measures for the execution of the intended final solution [*Endlösung*] of the Jewish question.

Göring

Source: Hermann Göring orders Reinhard Heydrich to prepare a plan for the 'Final Solution' of the 'Jewish problem', 31 July, 1941

4.3 The Wannsee Conference

The conference on the final solution [*Endlösung*] of the Jewish question held on January 20, 1942, in Berlin, Am Grossen Wannsee, No. 56–58.

The meeting opened with the announcement by the Chief of the Security Police and the SD, SS *Obergruppenführer* [General] Heydrich, of his appointment by the Reich Marshal as Plenipotentiary for the Preparation of the 'Final Solution' of the European Jewish Question. He noted that this Conference had been called in order to obtain clarity on questions of principle.

Responsibility for the handling of the final solution of the Jewish question, he said, would lie centrally with the *Reichsführer* [Field Marshal] SS and the Chief of the German Police (Chief of the Security Police and the SD), without regard to geographic boundaries.

The Chief of the Security Police and the SD then gave a brief review of the struggle conducted up to now against this foe.

The most important elements are:

a) Forcing the Jews out of the various areas of life [*Lebensgebiete*] of the German people.
b) Forcing the Jews out of the living space [*Lebensraum*] of the German people.

In pursuit of these aims, the accelerated emigration of the Jews from the area of the Reich, as the only possible provisional solution, was pressed forward and carried out according to plan.

On instructions by the Reich Marshal, a Reich Central Office for Jewish Emigration was set up in January 1939, and its direction entrusted to the Chief of the Security Police and the SD. Its tasks were, in particular:

a) To take all measures for the *preparation* of increased emigration of the Jews;
b) To *direct* the flow of emigration;
c) To speed up emigration in *individual* cases.

The aim of this task was to cleanse the German living space of Jews in a legal manner.

Source: Protocol of the Wannsee Conference, 20 January, 1942

Document case-study questions

1 Explain what is meant in these sources by a) the 'final solution' (4.2) and b) a 'Reich Central Office for Jewish Emigration' (4.3).

2 What can be learnt from 4.1 about Nazi plans in 1940 for the future of German Jewry?

3 In what ways does 4.2 show, by means of its tone and language, that it is an important statement on Nazi Jewish policy?

4 Noting the origins and content of 4.2, how valuable would it be for a historian studying the origins and implementation of the 'Final Solution'?

5 Comparing 4.2 and 4.3, what can be learnt about the role of Reinhard Heydrich in solving the 'Jewish question'?

6 From the evidence of these documents and your own knowledge, outline how, and why, Nazi policy for solving the 'Jewish question' changed between 1939 and 1942.

Notes and references

1 L. Dawidowicz, *The war against the Jews, 1933–45*, London, 1975, p. 138.

2 Dawidowicz, *War against the Jews*, p. 143.

3 Dawidowicz, *War against the Jews*, p. 148.

4 K. D. Bracher, *Zeitgeschichtliche Kontroversen. Um Faschismus, Totalitarianismus, Demokratie*, Munich, 1976, p. 62.

5 P. Burrin, *Hitler and the Jews*, London, 1994, p. 150.

6 Dawidowicz, *War against the Jews*, p. 176.

7 Burrin, *Hitler*, p. 129.

The killing machine

After the Nazis had taken the decision in the autumn of 1941 to annihilate the European Jews all that remained was to select the most appropriate instrument of killing. As discussed in Chapter 4, the selective gassing of Jews began at Chelmno in December 1941. (Gassing was chosen because it spared Himmler's SS men the 'unpleasantness' involved in shooting Jews in the back of the head and throwing their bodies into mass graves.) At the end of 1941, however, gassing was still a relatively novel procedure and it became evident that it would require death camps where people could be gassed in large numbers in a relatively short time. It should not be forgotten that pioneering murders of mentally and physically disabled people had already been carried out by Professor Victor Brack as part of Hitler's euthanasia programme in Germany; those unfortunate people had joined the Jews, Gypsies and homosexuals, among others, on the Nazis' list of those deemed 'unfit' to live in the German Reich.

The story of this chapter is therefore one of the Nazis' acceleration of the mass murder of Jews throughout occupied Europe, which culminated in the gassing of 400,000 Hungarian Jews between 1944 and 1945.

The death camps

On 27 March 1942 Goebbels wrote in his diary 'not much will remain of the Jews'. This was a prophetic statement, which proved to be only too tragically accurate, but it also reflected the confidence of the Nazi leadership that its new death camps would provide the means for the extermination of European Jewry.

These new camps became operational in 1942: Belzec in February; Sobibor and Auschwitz in March; and Majdanek and Treblinka by the early summer. All of these camps were in Poland, linked by rail to those parts of Europe that had been selected to send more and more Jews to their deaths.

The first party of Jewish victims from Slovakia was sent to Auschwitz in March, and Goebbels' diary reference noted the emptying of the Lublin ghetto at the end of that month. Transportations from the Warsaw ghetto to Treblinka, and the Lvov ghetto to Belzec, began in late July 1942.

By now, the Nazis had identified their most efficient chemical killing agent. This was Zyklon B gas, which had first been tried out on Soviet prisoners of war in the autumn of 1941 (because the USSR had not signed the Geneva Convention regulating the treatment of prisoners, captured Soviets were regarded as legitimate victims for Nazi 'experiments').

Figure 3. The location of the concentration camps, death camps and euthanasia centres.

By the late summer of 1942, the system was operating with smooth efficiency. Dutch and Croatian Jews were sent to Auschwitz, which became the main killing centre, and in November 1942 Jews from Norway arrived there. They were followed early in 1943 by Jews from Greece, shortly after Hitler had ordered, in February 1943, that all Jews should be expelled from Berlin (an indication that they were to be murdered). In February 1943, too, the Lvov ghetto was destroyed by the Nazis; later that year it was the turn of the ghettos in Minsk (in Byelorussia) and Vilna (in Lithuania).

And so the process of extermination went on. In October 1943 Danish Jews became the latest victims of the Nazi killing machine; this despite the courageous refusal of the Danish people, almost alone in Europe, to co-operate in the systematic rounding up of Jews so that they could be sent to their deaths.

The everyday reality of the death camps

It is natural for a contemporary reader to be numbed by the sheer enormity of the statistics that one is faced with when reading about the Holocaust. One's immediate response is to ask, firstly, how could human beings be capable of treating their fellow men, women and children in such a callous and murderous way? Secondly, how could anyone have survived such treatment, and what strategies did the Jews evolve to deal with the everyday horror that they faced?

The matter-of-fact way in which the Nazi mass murderers went about their business has been well documented. Rudolf Hoess, the camp commandant at Auschwitz, boasted about the 'improvements' that he had made in his camp:

> We had two SS doctors on duty at Auschwitz [Hoess told a post-war Allied interrogator] to examine the incoming transports of prisoners. These would be marched by one of the doctors, who would make spot decisions as they walked by. Those who were fit to work were sent into the camp. Others were sent immediately to the extermination camps. Children of tender years were invariably exterminated since by reason of their youth they were unable to work . . . another improvement we made over Treblinka was that at Treblinka they almost always knew that they were to be exterminated, while at Auschwitz we endeavoured to fool the victims into thinking that they were going through a delousing process.[1]

Sometimes Hoess and his SS colleagues faced inconveniences.

> Of course [he said], frequently they realized our true intentions and we sometimes had riots and difficulties. Very frequently women would hide their children under clothes but of course when we found them we would send them in to be exterminated. We were required to carry out these exterminations in secrecy, but of course the foul and nauseating stench from the continuous burning of bodies permeated the entire area and all of the people living in the surrounding communities knew that exterminations were going on at Auschwitz.[2]

Various significant points emerge from Hoess' account. Firstly, his pride in his work: Jews were deceived about their ultimate fate, and even when they became aware of it and tried to evade it they, or their children, were efficiently dealt with.

Hoess also makes it clear that people living in the surrounding area must have been aware of what was happening in Auschwitz. This point is perhaps of less significance with regard to Poland, where people were rarely complicit in the mass murder of Jews, than in Germany itself. Could the German people of Weimar, for example, have been unaware of the horrors being perpetrated in the nearby camp at Buchenwald? It was not one of the major death camps, but thousands of Jews and other people were murdered there nonetheless. Daniel Goldhagen[3] has argued that all Germans, regardless of their direct involvement in it, share a collective German guilt for the Holocaust (Hoess himself was executed by the Allied powers for war crimes). It should be noted that Goldhagen's views, which are focused on the concept of the 'collective responsibility' of the German people for the Holocaust, are controversial, and have been attacked by other historians.

The other important point in the Hoess account is the reference to children being 'unable to work'. For some Jews, death in the gas crematoria was preceded by their brutal exploitation as slave labourers of the Reich in places like Mauthausen in Austria. Auschwitz had its own labour camp at Birkenau, where people were forced to work in wretched conditions, all the time being aware of the smoke belching from the crematoria chimneys as more bodies were burnt.

Hoess was proud of the degree of deception practised at Auschwitz. So was the commandant at Treblinka, Franz Stangl, who boasted to a journalist in 1971 about how he had built a fake railway station at the camp with signs that pointed to places like Warsaw and Bialystok. All this was designed to create a sense of 'normality' for Jewish victims, so that, as in Hoess' words, the mass killings could 'take place in an atmosphere of the greatest possible calm'. Hoess even complained about his burden of work at Auschwitz, when 9,000 people were being gassed every day. Like many SS officials, Hoess was grossly corrupt, a point made vividly in the recent film version of Thomas Keneally's novel of 1982, *Schindler's list*. In this story, 1,100 Jews were saved by Oskar Schindler, a Sudeten German, who bribed the relevant SS officer concerned. It seems that even in this system of human slaughterhouses there were still 'good Germans' who remembered that they were human beings first rather than being primarily responsible to the Nazi regime.

The survivors' experience

Day-to-day life in the camps was both banal and terrible. At Auschwitz, for example, the crematoria were surrounded by well-kept lawns, and music was played as people were taken to their deaths. One survivor remembered that there was an orchestra of 'young and pretty girls all dressed in white blouses and navy-blue skirts'[4] who were chosen from among the camp inmates. Catchy tunes, like 'The merry widow', were played while the Nazis selected their victims for the gas chambers.

Everyday existence in the camps was like a living death. In Auschwitz, the prisoners' misery was worsened by the millions of fleas which fed off their skeletal frames (food rations were deliberately kept to a minimum). A survivor of Birkenau, Bernd Naumann, wrote later about how the camp was infested with rats: 'They gnawed not only at corpses but also at the seriously sick. I have pictures showing women near death being bitten by rats.' Repulsive and inadequate latrines served up to 300 people at one sitting, according to Naumann; 'Hunger and extreme want', he wrote, 'made them [the camp inmates] into animals.'[5]

Another Auschwitz survivor, Viktor Frankl,[6] who spent three years in the camp, noted the dreadful effects of starvation and dehumanisation on the camp's inmates. After their last layers of subcutaneous fat had vanished, Frankl recorded that people looked like skeletons covered only by skin and rags. Individuals'

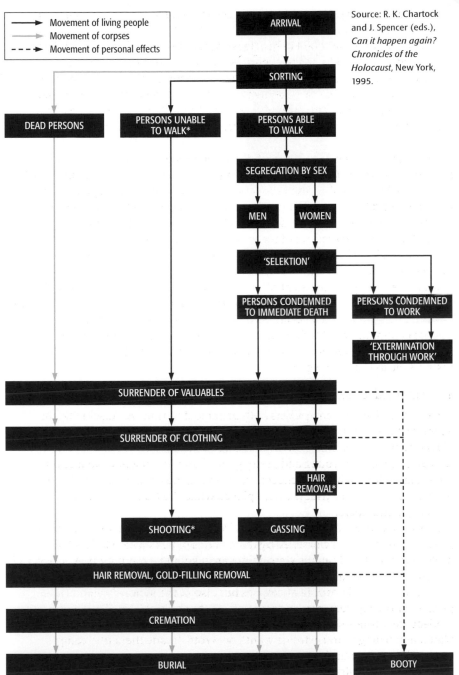

Legend:
- Movement of living people
- Movement of corpses
- Movement of personal effects

ARRIVAL

SORTING

DEAD PERSONS

PERSONS UNABLE TO WALK*

PERSONS ABLE TO WALK

SEGREGATION BY SEX

MEN

WOMEN

'SELEKTION'

PERSONS CONDEMNED TO IMMEDIATE DEATH

PERSONS CONDEMNED TO WORK

'EXTERMINATION THROUGH WORK'

SURRENDER OF VALUABLES

SURRENDER OF CLOTHING

HAIR REMOVAL*

SHOOTING*

GASSING

HAIR REMOVAL, GOLD-FILLING REMOVAL

CREMATION

BURIAL

BOOTY

Source: R. K. Chartock and J. Spencer (eds.), *Can it happen again? Chronicles of the Holocaust*, New York, 1995.

* Unique to Sobibor, Treblinka and Belzec

Figure 4. 'Operation Reinhard' (the Nazi codename for the extermination process in Sobibor, Belzec and Majdanek).

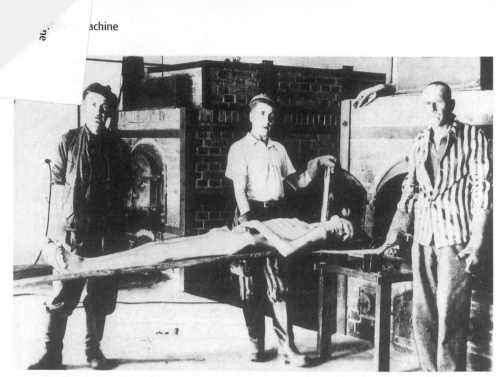

Auschwitz extermination camp inmates were forced to load the bodies of their fellow prisoners into ovens for cremation.

muscles disappeared as the body digested its own protein; ultimately, the body itself had no powers of resistance left, and one by one the members of Frankl's hut at Auschwitz died. The alternative to immediate gassing (invariably the fate of the very young and elderly) was therefore a painful, lingering death. Yet, as one observer noted, the normality of death in the camps 'caused death to lose its terror'.

Some Jews in camps like Auschwitz and Treblinka had the job of accompanying the victims to the gas chambers and, following their deaths, of disposing of the bodies after having extracted gold teeth, cut off hair and so on (the SS did not want to lose anything that might be of use for the Reich's war effort). These so-called *Sonderkommando* ('special commandos') had little choice but to perform these ghastly tasks; the alternative would have been to have been gassed themselves. Furthermore, normal standards of decency did not apply in the death camps, or, indeed, in the ghettos, like those in Warsaw and Lublin, from which the Jewish victims had come. A Jewish child in the Warsaw ghetto tellingly wrote 'I am hungry, I am cold; when I grow up I want to be a German, and then
I shall no longer be hungry, and no longer be cold.'

The problem of resistance

One of the apparent puzzles associated with the Holocaust is why there wasn't

One of a series of Nazi propaganda photographs taken inside the Warsaw ghetto in 1941. What impression of life in the ghetto is the Nazi photographer intending to present to the outside world with this image of starving Jewish children outside a well-stocked Jewish shop identified with a crudely drawn Star of David?

more resistance to its implementation. It is, however, extremely important to point out in the first instance that there was Jewish resistance in both the camps and the ghettos, most notably in the Warsaw ghetto in 1943. There were also other Jewish uprisings in Treblinka (August 1943), Sobibor (14 October 1943) and Chelmno (January 1945).

Jewish resistance groups

There was undoubtedly a generational difference within the Jewish community about the issue of resistance. The Germans manipulated the *Judenrate* (the Jewish councils) in the ghettos in order both to control the Jews and to select those people who were going to the camps. With hindsight, it is easy to be critical of the elders of the Jewish community for apparently co-operating with the Nazis, but in reality they had no choice: a refusal to co-operate could have resulted in a worsening of the already appalling conditions in the ghettos or death for the council members.

The older Jews who represented their communities on the *Judenrate* regarded resistance to the Nazis as both dangerous and pointless. By adopting this attitude they represented the traditional view of the Jewish leaders who saw it as their task to preserve their people in the face of anti-Semitic persecution. Plainly, however, there was little comparison between the pogroms of Tsarist Russia early in the twentieth century and the systematic mass murder of the Jews in the Third Reich.

Younger Jews, particularly those who were communists or Zionists, saw matters differently. Jewish communists regarded the murder of their people as a manifestation of the fascist evil against which they were struggling in Europe, while Zionists believed that Jewish honour and integrity demanded that the Nazi tyranny be resisted. Such beliefs led to tensions in the ghettos and camps between the younger and older generations.

The Warsaw uprising

The most dramatic example of Jewish resistance to the Nazi regime took place in Warsaw in 1943. It followed the decision taken by Himmler in February 1943 that the Warsaw ghetto should be destroyed. This decision provoked an uprising which lasted from 19 April to 15 May as the desperate Jewish defenders of the ghetto took refuge in the sewers underneath the city before finally being forced to surrender. Even the Nazis were surprised by the ferocity of the Jewish resistance.

Some Jews managed to escape from the ghetto and subsequently joined the Polish resistance. Such Jewish and Polish co-operation against Nazism posed problems in itself, for during the inter-war period anti-Semitism was strong in Poland. Jewish resisters were not always welcomed by the Polish resistance, while some Poles were overtly hostile to Jews and were prepared to collaborate with the Nazis in their persecution (as was the case in almost every country occupied by German forces). By contrast, by hiding them, other Poles took great risks in order to help Jews escape persecution (a celebrated example was the case of the film director Roman Polanski, who was hidden by two Polish peasants

Captured Jewish male and female fighters in the rubble of the Warsaw ghetto. Their heroic uprising was the first significant revolt against the Nazis in occupied Europe and encouraged the resistance movement in other ghettos and in concentration camps.

and survived the war).

Jewish culture

A remarkable feature of the Jewish experience under Nazism was the way in which the Jewish culture and language were preserved in the ghettos. The Jews set up special ghetto schools, in which Yiddish (the Jewish vernacular language) was taught, together with Jewish history, Hebrew and other academic subjects. Such courses, which in some instances included vocational subjects as well, attracted as many as 4,000 students alone in the Warsaw ghetto between 1940 and 1941. Lucy Dawidowicz writes that such ghetto schools 'provided the ghetto children with shelter, physical warmth, medical and sanitary care, food and emotional security'.[7] When the Jews were in the clutches of the killing machine at Auschwitz and other camps it proved impossible to continue such educational activities.

One of the most searing testimonies to the experience of Jewish children in the Holocaust can be seen in a museum attached to the Jewish cemetery in Prague, in the Czech Republic, where children's drawings of the Theresienstadt camp are preserved. (Ironically, Theresienstadt was supposed to be a 'model' camp, the only one into which foreign observers were allowed; the reality was that it was only a stopping place for Jews before they were sent to Treblinka or Auschwitz.) The innocent reality of the Theresienstadt drawings is separated by only days, or weeks, from the certainty of the children's death in the gas chambers.

The Hungarian Jews

The last, terrible phase of the Holocaust started in March 1944 with the effective occupation of Hungary by German forces. The Hungarian dictator, Miklós Horthy, resisted the German demands for the transportation of the 400,000 Hungarian Jews to the camps, but he was overridden. The job of organising the Jews' mass murder fell to Himmler's efficient henchman, Eichmann, who was assisted in his task by the local fascist organisation, the Arrow Cross Party.

Some Hungarian Jews were forced to march to Auschwitz, a considerable distance away, in Poland; many died on the way. Those who reached Auschwitz were gassed. In all, 70 per cent of the pre-war Jewish population in Hungary perished in the Holocaust.

Conclusion

It is difficult for historians, who are writing long after the event, to portray the true horror of the Holocaust. The author visited Buchenwald on a bright August day, where he realised that the piles of the murdered victims' shoes, spectacles and clothes, along with other stolen items on display, could only give a superficial understanding of this human catastrophe.

It is, in fact, amazing that some individuals were able to rise above the horror of the Holocaust and were able to underline by personal example the fact that human values and civilisation could survive the crimes of the Nazis. Two stories serve to illustrate this. One concerns the Dutch Jewish girl, Anne Frank, who hid in her family's house in Amsterdam for years before being betrayed to the Nazis. Anne Frank would ultimately die in a death camp, yet before she was captured she could still write in her diary of her belief 'that peace and tranquillity will return'.[8] The other story involves Raoul Wallenberg, one of those whom the Jewish people call 'righteous Gentiles' (sadly a heroic minority) who went out of their way to help the Jews. Wallenberg, a Swedish diplomat, saved the lives of hundreds of Hungarian Jews by issuing them with Swedish passports in Budapest. Tragically, it is believed that Wallenberg died in a Soviet prison as a result of his life-saving actions having been misinterpreted by another tyrannical regime.

Finally, however, we are left with the evidence of the overwhelming scale of the Nazis' genocide of the Jews between 1939 and 1945: 6 million Jews died in the camps or elsewhere in Hitler's attempt to realise his racist fantasy of a 'Jew-free' Europe.

The death camps and ghettos

5.1 Himmler demands secrecy about the Holocaust

I also want to speak very frankly about an extremely important subject. Among ourselves we will discuss it openly; in public however, we must never mention it . . . I mean the evacuations of the Jews, the extermination of Jewish people.

Source: Heinrich Himmler, 1942, quoted in R. K. Chartock and J. Spencer (eds.), *Can it happen again? Chronicles of the Holocaust*, New York, 1995, p. 169

5.2 A Nazi tries to defend his actions

I took part in the murder of many people . . . I believed in the *Führer*, I wanted to serve my people. Today I know that this idea was false. I regret the mistakes of my past, but I cannot undo them.

Source: Hans Stark, a former member of the Gestapo staff at Auschwitz camp, quoted in P. Friedmann, *Martyrs and fighters*, Connecticut, 1954

5.3 The Warsaw-ghetto uprising, 1943

We couldn't resist the bombing, especially their method of setting fire to the ghetto. All life vanished from the streets and houses. We hid in the cellars and bunkers. From there we made our sorties. We went out at night. The Germans were in the ghetto mostly by day, leaving at night. They were afraid to enter the ghetto at night. If you could lick my heart, it would poison you.

Source: Itzak Zuchermann and Simha Rottem, quoted in Claude Lanzmann, *Shoah*, 1985, and in R. K. Chartock and J. Spencer (eds.), *Can it happen again? Chronicles of the Holocaust*, New York, 1995, p. 25

5.4 The activities of Reserve Police Battalion 101 in occupied Poland

The market place filled rapidly with Jews, including mothers with infants. While the men of Reserve Police Battalion 101 were apparently willing to shoot those Jews too weak or sick to move, they still shied for the most part from shooting infants, despite their orders.

Source: C. Browning, *The path to genocide*, Cambridge, 1992, p. 175

5.5 The significance of the labour camps

The entire camp structure underwent significant changes in 1942, as the German war effort bogged down and the demand for labour increased. Gradually the camps were seen as pools of forced labour in addition to being part of the terror apparatus of the regime.

Source: M. Marrus, *The Holocaust in history*, London, 1987, p. 127

Document case-study questions

1 Explain the need for secrecy about the Holocaust referred to by Himmler in 5.1.

2 In what ways do the accounts of Nazi behaviour in 5.2 and 5.4 contrast with one another?

3 What does 5.3 tell us about the nature and extent of Jewish resistance in the Warsaw ghetto in 1943?

4 Refer to 5.5; what explanation does this source provide for the differing demands put on the camps after 1942?

5 Can Jews be accused of failing to resist the Holocaust? Justify your conclusions with reference to 5.3.

Notes and references

1 'Hoess explains why he killed the Jews', in R. K. Chartock and J. Spencer (eds.), *Can it happen again? Chronicles of the Holocaust*, New York, 1995.

2 W. Shirer, 'The death house', in Chartock and Spencer, *Can it?*, p. 29.

3 D. Goldhagen, *Hitler's willing executioners. Ordinary Germans and the Holocaust*, London, 1996.

4 Shirer, 'Death house'.

5 B. Naumann, 'The horrors of daily life', in Chartock and Spencer, *Can it?*, p. 31.

6 V. Frankl, *Man's search for meaning*, 1959.

7 L. Dawidowicz, *The war against the Jews, 1933–45*, London, 1975, p. 311.

8 B. Wilkomirski, *Fragments: A. Frank, the diary of a young girl*, New York, 1952.

6 The foreign reaction to the Holocaust

So far this study has focused on the Jewish experience of the Holocaust and has attempted to provide some sort of perspective on the Nazis' anti-Semitic policies. Another important aspect of the Holocaust, however, is the reaction of the outside world to the events occurring in the Third Reich. How much was known in countries like Britain and the United States about the Nazis' mass murder of the Jews? When was the Holocaust first known about and how did foreign governments react to the information that they received about it? The failure of democratic governments, in particular, to take reports of the Holocaust seriously is one of the most alarming aspects of the history of the 'Final Solution'.

The foreign reaction to the Nazi accession to power

During the 1920s, the Nazi Party was an obscure, and not very successful, party on the political fringe. This changed, however, as a result of Hitler's relentless drive for power between 1930 and 1933. By 1932 the NSDAP had become the most popular political party in Germany and therefore had to be taken seriously, but there was still a tendency in other countries to regard it as consisting of frustrated nationalists who would moderate their views after their grievances had been addressed. Nevertheless, some very accurate analyses of what Nazism stood for were made by contemporary foreign observers, notably by the retiring British ambassador in Berlin, Sir Horace Rumbold, in 1933 (see document 6.2).

Some foreign leaders had taken the trouble to read *Mein Kampf*, but few took its message seriously, despite the growing evidence of Nazi thuggery. As early as 8 April 1933 the *Manchester Guardian* reported on how a Jew had been beaten to death by Brownshirts in Silesia; in its story it further concluded that 'Any German who dares say a true word about the terror in his own country runs the risk of a fearful beating, or long imprisonment or even death.'

Accurate, on-the-spot reporting about what was happening in Germany went hand in hand with a naive acceptance of Nazi propaganda. In the United States, for example, the celebrated aviator Charles Lindbergh was a strong admirer of the 'new' Germany and had counterparts in Britain, like Lord Lothian and Lord Winterton. In both France and Britain there were also active fascist organisations whose programmes were strongly anti-Semitic. The leader of the British Union of Fascists (BUF), Sir Oswald Mosley, was a greater admirer of Mussolini than of

Hitler (Mussolini's vision for Italy did not generally include racist policies), but he still did nothing to prevent the BUF from assuming a racist position, while, in France, the *Action Française* was rabidly anti-Jewish. In the USA, too, the German–American *Bund* ('union'), the John Birch Society and the Ku Klux Klan were all fascist-style organisations with strong anti-Semitic platforms.

Anti-Jewish prejudice

One of the reasons why the Western democracies did not react more strongly to reported events in Germany was that Jews were often perceived to be 'alien' and somehow 'un-British' or 'un-American'. In Britain, what is often described as 'golf-club anti-Semitism' (whereby Jews were excluded from social and sporting organisations like golf and tennis clubs) was quite widespread among the upper classes. More seriously, anti-Semitism also pervaded government circles: thus Lord Halifax, the foreign secretary from 1938 to 1940, admitted to being 'mildly anti-Semitic', while his predecessor in office, Anthony Eden, was described by his private secretary as being 'hopelessly prejudiced against Jews'.[1]

In Eden's case, his prejudice was influenced by his pro-Arabism. Britain was the colonial power in Palestine during the inter-war period and had encouraged Jews to settle there with its 1917 Balfour Declaration. Unsurprisingly, however, Arabs in Palestine objected to such an influx of Jews and Britain was faced with a serious uprising of the Palestinian Arabs in 1936. Eden, who was foreign secretary from 1935 to 1938, was a fluent Arab speaker whose sympathy for the Arab world made him regard the Jews as a nuisance. Like others in the Foreign Office he was reluctant to take the horrific evidence about the Holocaust seriously.[2]

Such prejudices would prove to be significant when the first stories about the unfolding Holocaust reached the Foreign Office in London. There was also resistance to exploring the implications of the reports of the Nazis' anti-Semitic policies in the US State Department in Washington, DC.

Kristallnacht

There were, however, some differences of nuance in Anglo-American attitudes to what was happening in Nazi Germany. President F. D. Roosevelt's reaction to the events of *Kristallnacht* in 1938 was to withdraw the US ambassador to Germany in protest; for its part, Britain did not do the same, even though leading members of the government, like Halifax, claimed to have been shocked by the burning of synagogues. Yet Britain did accept 40,000 German Jews in the aftermath of *Kristallnacht*, while the United States made no such gesture (tellingly, an opinion poll taken at the time revealed that four-fifths of all Americans opposed allowing any more German-Jewish migrants to settle in their country).

Although Roosevelt convened the Evian Conference in France in 1939 on the question of Jewish refugees, his action has been castigated by some historians as a cosmetic one. The official annual quota of 30,000 Jewish migrants to the USA remained in place, almost certainly because Roosevelt did not want to antagonise US isolationists who regarded any official act of sympathy towards German Jews as evidence that the USA might get involved in a European war against Germany. The isolationists also held right-wing, anti-Semitic views which Roosevelt, who was anxious to be re-elected as president in 1940, dared not openly oppose. Roosevelt was no anti-Semite, but like all American presidents he had to maintain a delicate political balance. As late as 1940 US public opinion was still strongly isolationist and this factor over-rode any influence that the Jewish-American community might have had on US policy.

The Hore-Belisha scandal

The extent to which latent anti-Semitism existed in Britain was demonstrated when the war minister, Leslie Hore-Belisha (a Jew), was sacked from Neville Chamberlain's wartime government in January 1940. Not only was Hore-Belisha disliked by the generals, who did not like the way in which he was trying to reform the British army, but there was also clear evidence that Lord Halifax was prejudiced against him. A 'vicious whispering campaign' was instigated against Hore-Belisha, culminating in his removal from office, even though he was a dynamic and effective minister.[3]

The dismissal of Hore-Belisha showed that there was active anti-Jewish prejudice in British governmental circles. This was not remotely comparable to the vicious racism encouraged by the Nazis in Germany, but it nevertheless made certain British government leaders (with notable exceptions, like Winston Churchill, who was resolutely pro-Zionist) less sympathetic to the Jewish cause than they could have been.

Anti-Semitism in France

Such British political anti-Semites were not the only ones. The slogan of the French political right during the late 1930s was 'Better Hitler than Blum' (a reference to Léon Blum, France's Jewish socialist prime minister from 1936 to 1937 and again in 1938). The viciousness of French anti-Semitism was shown when the Vichy regime, led by Marshal Philippe Pétain, came to power in June 1940, following the signing of an armistice with Germany. The Vichy regime collaborated with the Nazis, passing legislation – a carbon copy of that enacted in Germany – against the Jews and even co-operating in the rounding-up of French Jews, who were subsequently sent to death camps.

When the Allies knew

Documentation that has recently been made available in the Public Record Office in London makes it clear that the British knew about the Nazis' extermination of the Jews in the USSR in 1941. (This information was obtained by the British Code and Cypher School at Bletchley Park, which monitored wartime Nazi communications.)

The British government's failure to react to such information has been defended by some on the grounds that to have responded would have alerted the Germans to the success of the codebreaking exercise, which would have jeopardised the Allied war effort. Another argument is that at that time such stories might have been regarded as propaganda, as new versions of the anti-German atrocity stories that had circulated during the First World War (which were long denied, but in some instances are now known to have been true).

The Allies also had other sources of information regarding the Nazis' anti-Jewish atrocities. In May 1942, for example, Jan Karski, a representative of the Polish underground resistance in Warsaw, arrived in London with a report which told the British government of the way in which the Jews in Poland were being systematically liquidated. The information made available by Karski was actually broadcast by the BBC on 2 June 1942, and again later in the month, yet the government showed no signs of reacting to the news from Poland or the USSR.

The Riegner telegram

On 10 August 1942 the Foreign Office in London received a telegram from its consul-general in Geneva, in neutral Switzerland. It contained a message from Gerhart Riegner, the secretary of the World Jewish Congress, which was supposed to be passed on to the Jewish Labour MP Sidney Silverman. The telegram read:

> Receiving alarming reports stating that, in the *Führer*'s Headquarters, a plan has been discussed, and is under consideration, according to which all Jews in countries occupied or controlled by Germany numbering three-and-a-half to four millions should, after deportation and concentration in the East, be at one blow exterminated.[4]

In fact, as we now know, the process of the mass murder of the Jews had been decided upon at least a year before, and the gas ovens at Treblinka and Auschwitz had been at work for months when Riegner's telegram arrived. Riegner's telegram was really an account of the Wannsee Conference of January 1942; nevertheless, it presented the Foreign Office with an accurate appraisal of the Nazis' intentions towards the Jews. A Foreign Office lawyer, however, minuted the comment 'We should not help matters by taking any further action on the basis of this rather wild story.'

The foreign secretary, Anthony Eden (who had been reappointed to the position in 1940), saw no reason for holding a House of Commons debate about such Nazi 'atrocity stories' when Silverman asked for one. Silverman was furthermore prevented from telephoning Rabbi Stephen Wise, the head of the American Jewish Congress, about Riegner's telegram. Only on 28 August 1942 did the information contained in the telegram reach the United States, and even then the US State Department persuaded Wise not to publicise the information given about the Nazis' plans until it could be confirmed. It was not until November 1942 that the US public learned of the contents of the telegram, and by then millions of Jews had already perished.

The Vatican

The Catholic Church was one of the most influential organisations in Europe. It, too, was well informed – and perhaps better informed than the governments of the Western democracies – about the Nazis' atrocities in occupied Poland (Poland was, after all, one of the most devoutly Catholic states on the whole of the European continent). Yet Pope Pius XII remained silent, making no statement condemning the Nazi persecution of the Jews (by contrast, his predecessor, Pius XI, had attacked Nazism in 1937). How do we account for this striking failure? In part, it was a reflection of the age-old tension between Judaism and Catholicism, but it also owed something to the personality and experience of Pius XII himself.

Pius was undoubtedly a conscientious man who believed that his policy regarding the Jews was a correct one. He decided to refrain from making a public condemnation of Nazi anti-Semitism for fear that the situation of the Jews (as well as of his own co-religionists, whose devotion to the Catholic Church was not encouraged by the Nazis) would become worse if he spoke out. Pius has been condemned for his decision by both Jews and many non-Jews. How, historians have not unreasonably asked in retrospect, could the situation of the Jews under the Nazi regime have become any worse than it already was?

Three factors appear to have influenced Pius XII's decision. Firstly, he had been the papal nuncio (papal ambassador) in Germany for many years before he became pope in 1939, which meant that he was naturally sympathetic to, and reluctant to condemn, Germany. Secondly, like most members of the hierarchy of the Catholic Church, he regarded communism as a greater threat to Catholicism than Nazism. Thus, as one historian has written, the

> theory that Germany was the bastion of Europe contributed largely to that ambivalent attitude which prevented Pacelli (Pope Pius XII from 1939) from issuing a public condemnation of National Socialism during the war.[5]

Their assumption that fascism was acceptable as a counterweight to communism put both the Catholic and Protestant churches in a false, and arguably ultimately immoral, position. The third point about the pope's attitude towards Nazi anti-Semitism is that he was alarmed by events that had occurred in The Netherlands (then under German occupation) in 1940, when leading members of the Catholic hierarchy had spoken out against the Nazis' persecution of Jewish converts to Catholicism and the Nazis had retaliated by sending dozens of them to camps. Pius XII appears to have thought that the number of Jewish converts involved was much larger, but his anxiety to avoid a similar situation precluded, his defenders argue, his making any public statement on the subsequent Nazi persecution of the Jews.

There is evidence that the pope may have approved the protection of some Hungarian Jews by the papal nuncio in Budapest, but the numbers of Jews involved were small, especially in relation to the hundreds of thousands who died between 1944 and 1945. Pius XII's critics have continued to argue that he failed in his moral duty as the leader of the largest Christian church by remaining silent about the Nazis' persecution of the Jews. They point to the example of the German bishop of Münster, August von Galen, who openly attacked the Nazi euthanasia policy in 1941 and was not arrested because the Nazis were intimidated by his popularity. It is, however, fair to point out that the Nazis merely carried on their euthanasia programme in secret, despite the Catholic bishop's attack on it (the SS's obsession with secrecy with regard to the Holocaust has already been discussed).

The Protestant churches

A brief discussion of the attitudes of the Protestant churches to Nazism is relevant here. Broadly speaking, there were three positions adopted by Protestants within Germany.

1 Some Protestants were out-and-out supporters of the Nazis and joined their so-called 'Reich Church'.
2 Other Protestants kept a low profile, making no public criticism of Nazi policy.
3 A heroic Protestant minority, led by men like Pastor Dietrich Bonhoeffer, set up the so-called 'Confessing Church', which condemned the persecution of the Jews in 1943.

The Confessing Church was supported, as was the anti-Nazi resistance of which Bonhoeffer was a member, by concerned Protestant clergy abroad, like the bishop of Chichester, George Bell, in England.

Overall, however, the impression remains that both the Catholic and Protestant church leaders, inside and outside Germany, did not adopt a strong enough position against Nazi racism. This position contrasts with the heroic self-sacrifice of individuals like Bonhoeffer and the Catholic priest Alfred Delp, who both died resisting Nazism. The Catholic Church, in particular, has since been reluctant to admit to any error on its part regarding the conduct of its wartime policy towards the Jews; this attitude has continued to cause offence to Jewish people.

War crimes

One of the questions which arose on the Allied side during the Second World War was what should be done with those in Germany who were guilty of crimes against humanity once the war had been won by the Allies. In a broadcast on 22 June 1941, the day that the German army invaded the USSR, the British prime minister, Winston Churchill, threatened retribution, not only against the Nazis, but also against those who had collaborated with them in occupied Europe. Such offenders, Churchill warned, 'will be delivered by us on the morrow of the victory to the justice of the Allied tribunals'.

The Foreign Office was decidedly unenthusiastic about the prospective prosecution of war criminals; it also continued to greet the 'stream of atrocity reports from Western Europe . . . with scepticism'.[6] When more alarming reports came through from Europe (such as that regarding the massacre of 34,000 Ukrainian Jews at Babi-Yar in 1941), they were dismissed as products of the 'Slovak imagination'. Even when it was acknowledged that such reports might have some credibility, a Foreign Office official noted that trying to hunt down Nazi war criminals after the war would be 'virtually impossible'. It was better, in the Foreign Office's view, to leave the Germans to the vengeance of their neighbours rather than adopt any systematic system for dealing with the perpetrators of the Nazis' war crimes.

The Foreign Office was forced to assume a different viewpoint when President Roosevelt made a statement condemning Nazi atrocities on 25 October 1941 and Churchill (who was anxious to court the then neutral USA) promised 'retribution for these crimes'. The British suspicion of Soviet Russia, despite their alliance following the German invasion of the Soviet Union, meant that the Soviet leader, Josef Stalin, was not consulted about the setting-up of a war-crimes commission.

When the United States entered the war in December 1941, neither the US secretary of state for foreign affairs, Cordell Hull, nor the State Department showed much enthusiasm for prosecuting Nazi war criminals. It was suggested that such a process might divert much-needed resources from the Allied war effort.

The Allied powers' unwillingness to accept the available evidence about Nazi atrocities against the Jews was compounded by an Anglo-American reluctance to act after the evidence became overwhelming. This was, perhaps, not surprising, given that in British governmental circles there was scepticism about the reports of SS massacres of British prisoners of war in 1940, even though the reports were made by repatriated British prisoners. It seems that officials who would not believe their own countrymen could find plenty of excuses for not believing 'wild stories' about the fate of the Jews in occupied Europe, and any suggestions that all members of the Gestapo should be arrested were rejected out of hand.

The Hungarian Jews

When it came to the fate of the Hungarian Jews in 1944 the Allied powers could not pretend to be ignorant of what was happening. The Jewish Agency for Palestine had long been begging the British government that Hungarian Jews should be allowed to go to Palestine (see Chapter 3). This plea was refused. The British priority was to appease the Palestinian-Arab population and the British government had produced a white paper in 1939 which enforced an annual quota of the number of Jews who were allowed to emigrate to Palestine; in 1944 such emigration would stop altogether. When a Hungarian Jew called Joel Brand arrived in Turkey with an offer from Eichmann, who was now trying to save his neck in the event of an Allied victory, that all the Hungarian Jews would be released in exchange for tons of coffee, tea, cocoa and soap, as well as 10,000 trucks, Brand was arrested on suspicion of being a Gestapo spy. Nothing came of Eichmann's offer and he continued deporting Jews to Poland.

An emotional response to the plight of the Hungarian Jews on the part of the US public did, however, force the British to issue 5,000 immigration certificates for Palestine to Hungarian Jews. The US government also supported Raoul Wallenberg's campaign to save the Jews in Budapest; tragically, however, the Soviets perceived Wallenberg as a US agent and he was imprisoned when the Red army occupied Budapest in 1945.

The fate of the Hungarian Jews also appalled officials in the US Department of War, who put pressure on the reluctant diplomats to take action against the Nazis' war crimes. Reluctantly, too, the Foreign Office in London was forced to draw up a 'list of those whose crimes would be so notorious to the conscience of mankind that their fate decided by political decision would not only be accepted, but expected'. Even then, there were arguments about whether German generals and industrialists should be included on a list of war criminals. In London, the whole issue of war crimes was surrounded by muddle, obfuscation and ill will. By the end of 1944 'it was clear to everyone except the Foreign Office that the half-hearted British attempt to organise a war crimes policy . . . was a hopeless failure'.[7] It was the Americans who would take the initiative.

Conclusion

The record of the Anglo-American democracies with regard to the unfolding of the Holocaust is not an impressive one; neither is that of the Christian churches. Prejudice, sloth and a lack of imagination weakened or negated any efforts to assist the endangered Jewish population of occupied Europe. The Riegner telegram, as Marrus[8] points out, did not convey an entirely accurate picture of what was happening in Europe (or, indeed, of what had already happened), but it should nevertheless have set alarm bells ringing. The fact that messages like this were initially treated with such scepticism and were subsequently followed by an unwillingness to act is a telling judgement on the nature of the governmental circles of the time.

Certainly, the Holocaust was shrouded in a cloak of secrecy by the Nazis, and the historian Martin Gilbert may well be right in his suggestion that it was only in mid-1944, following the escape of four Jews from Auschwitz, that the awful truth about Auschwitz become clear. Yet the BBC, the British press and, to a lesser degree, the American press, had earlier carried reports on Nazi atrocities and massacres of Jews, and by 1942 sufficient information was available to precipitate those politicians, like Churchill, who were sympathetic to the Jewish cause, into action. Sadly, they were always in a minority.

Contemporary foreign reaction to the Holocaust

6.1 The British reaction to Nazism

The German nation as a whole possesses, in a mental and physical sense, a virility and determination which has seldom, if ever, been exceeded in the world's history. No one who has any friendship with individual Germans, as I have, can doubt that. See the German boys in school: see the German young men and women: see the magnificent physique and determination of these people . . . her grievances arising from the Versailles Treaty, are in her judgement, still unredressed.

Source: Lord Winterton, speech to the House of Lords, 1935

6.2 Sir Horace Rumbold on Nazi anti-Semitism

On every Jew shop was plastered a large notice warning the public not to buy in Jewish shops. In many cases, special notices were put up saying that sweated labour was employed in that particular shop and often you saw a caricature of Jewish noses. It was utterly cruel and Hunnish the whole thing, just doing down a heap of defenceless people.

Source: Sir Horace Rumbold, in a letter to his mother, 2 April 1933, quoted in M. Gilbert, *Sir Horace Rumbold*, London, 1973, p. 375

6.3 The Evian Conference

Eventually, in what was described as a tawdry public relations move, President Roosevelt called for an international conference on the Jewish refugee problem. It convened at Evian les Bains, the old French spa, between 6 July and 14 July 1939, but the results were zero. No one agreed to accept immigrants from Nazi Germany. Each government, beset with its own economic ills, was fearful of adding foreigners to its population. Eventually, only the British admitted about 40,000. Franklin Roosevelt, who called the Conference, also refused to antagonize his domestic opponents, the isolationists.

Source: J. Weitz, *Joachim von Ribbentrop. Hitler's diplomat*, London, 1992, p. 183

6.4 The Prussian Confessing Church condemns the Holocaust, October 1943

The divine order knows no such terms as 'exterminate', 'liquidate' or 'useless life'. Extermination of men simply because they are relatives of a criminal, are old, or mentally defective or members of a foreign race is not 'a use of the sword which is the prerogative of authority' . . . We cannot allow our responsibility before God to be taken from us by our superiors.

Source: K. D. Bracher, 'Problems of the German resistance', in H. Bull (ed.), *The challenge of the Third Reich*, Oxford, 1986, p.66

6.5 The Holocaust: problems of belief

One reads these accounts again and again – and yet there remains the instinct to disbelieve, to question, to doubt. There is less of a mental barrier in accepting the weirdest stories of supernatural phenomena as, for example, running water uphill and trees with roots reaching to the sky, than in taking at face value these narratives which go beyond the frontiers of human cruelty and savagery.

Source: *Trials of war criminals before the Nuremberg Military Tribunals, 1947–49*, IV, p. 450

Document case-study questions

1 What can be learned about the author's attitude to Nazi anti-Semitism from 6.2?

2 In what ways does Rumbold's attitude in 6.2 contrast with that of Winterton in 6.1?

3 Using what you have read in this chapter and the material in 6.3, account for the US attitude towards the Jewish-refugee problem at the time of the Evian Conference in 1939.

4 In what ways does the Prussian Confessional Church show its disapproval of Nazi anti-Semitic policy in 6.4?

5 How does the evidence of 6.5 and the other four documents help to explain the apparent indifference of the Anglo-American governments and the Vatican to the fate of European Jewry in the Holocaust?

Notes and references

1 J. Harvey (ed.), *The war diaries of Oliver Harvey*, London, 1978, p. 194.

2 T. Bower, *Blind eye to murder*, London, 1981, pp. 36–37.

3 A. Roberts, *The holy fox. A biography of Lord Halifax*, London, 1991, p. 191.

4 *Punishment for war crimes*, vol. 2, p. 8, FO 371/30918/8472, PRO, quoted in Bower, *Blind eye*, p. 43.

5 K. D. Bracher, 'Problems of the German resistance', in H. Bull (ed.), *The challenge of the Third Reich*, Oxford, 1986, p. 68.

6 Bower, *Blind eye*, p. 34.

7 Bower, *Blind eye*, p. 84.

8 M. Marrus, *The Holocaust in history*, London, 1987, p. 161.

7 The Holocaust deniers

In view of the overwhelming amount of documentary and archive-film evidence about the Holocaust, it may seem extraordinary that any post-war historians or writers should attempt to deny that the Holocaust ever happened. Yet there has been a plethora of such analysts during the post-war period, particularly in the USA. Among such analysts, the outright denial of the Holocaust has been accompanied either by attempts to play down the horror of the Holocaust by saying, for example, that the number of Jews that were killed has been exaggerated, or by a so-called 'relativist' approach, whereby the Holocaust is regarded as being no worse than such Allied 'atrocities' as the bombing of the German city of Dresden in 1945.

Holocaust denial in the United States

The existence of far-right organisations which were strongly anti-Jewish and isolationist in the United States before the Second World War has been referred to in Chapter 6. During the post-war period, neo-fascist proponents have spawned a virtual industry of Holocaust deniers and relativists, with Holocaust denial frequently being combined with relativism.

H. Elmer Barnes

The 'father' of the post-war Holocaust deniers in the USA was H. Elmer Barnes, a sociologist who initially sympathised with the German people's grievances regarding the Treaty of Versailles. Barnes subsequently moved from this position to become an apologist for the Nazi regime, and by 1962 was questioning whether the Third Reich had, in fact, committed any atrocities at all.

Barnes claimed that the fact that Western leaders had tried to reach an accommodation with Hitler during the 1930s was proof that Hitler had been 'demonised' by the West only after Germany had lost the war. Barnes initially claimed that the number of Jews who had been killed in the Holocaust had been exaggerated, before later adopting a position of denying that the gas chambers had ever existed.

Barnes believed that it was the Allies, not Germany, who were responsible for starting the Second World War, and he adopted a relativist position on the Holocaust as well.

It is almost alarmingly easy [Barnes claimed] to demonstrate that the atrocities of the Allies in the same period were more numerous as to the victims, and were carried out for the most part by methods more brutal and painful than alleged extermination in gas ovens.[1]

His use of the word 'alleged' in the above quotation categorises Barnes as a classic Holocaust denier, who uses relativism as an additional weapon in his offensive armoury. Barnes argued that any Nazi anti-Jewish atrocities that may have been committed were less horrific than those perpetrated by the Allies in their bombing of Dresden, in Germany, and Hiroshima and Nagasaki, in Japan.

When the West German government wanted to compensate Jews after 1945 for their treatment under the Nazi regime, Barnes accused it of masochistic behaviour. Like other deniers of the Holocaust, he was angered by West Germany's requests for forgiveness by Israel, the Jewish state. Essentially, however, as perhaps the most prominent historian of Holocaust denial, Deborah Lipstadt, has pointed out, 'The roots of Barnes' views about the Holocaust . . . can be found in his anti-Semitism.'[2] It was Barnes' prejudice against Jews, Lipstadt believes, which can be said to underlie his attempt to explain away the Holocaust. Yet Barnes himself claimed that his critics were trying to smear him as being an anti-Semite because they could not refute his version of history.

Arthur R. Butz

Arthur R. Butz was another leading Holocaust denier in the USA. In his book, *The hoax of the twentieth century*,[3] Butz claimed that the gas chambers had never existed because there had never been any German attempt to exterminate the Jews. According to Butz, the death camps were, in fact, transit camps or ghettos, to which Jews were sent for their own safety when the Red army was nearing the Eastern Front.

Butz was a former lecturer in electrical engineering and computer science at Northwestern University in Evanston, Illinois; like Barnes, he therefore had no proper credentials as a historian. Although Lucy Dawidowicz describes Butz's book as 'clearly the product of an unhinged mind',[4] Butz was sponsored by the Liberty Lobby, the biggest and richest anti-Jewish organisation in the USA. It was the Liberty Lobby which financed the Institute for Historical Review, an anti-Semitic organisation; the institute even published a journal, the *Journal of Historical Review*, in an attempt to promote its efforts to achieve academic legitimacy.

Other US Holocaust deniers

Following the lead of Barnes and Butz, even more Holocaust-denial theorists appeared in the USA. James Madole, for example, claimed in 1959 that there were only 600,000 German Jews, so that 6 million Jews could not have died in the Holocaust (his refusal to accept the fact that European Jews had died was thus glaringly revealed). In 1959 Benjamin H. Freedman claimed that because

American Jews had refused to answer a census question about their religious affiliation it could be construed that the 6 million supposedly 'missing' European Jews (who had, in fact, died in the Holocaust) had been living in the USA. During the 1970s one Holocaust denier, Austin App, claimed that the Holocaust was an 'impudent lie', while another, William Grimstad, said that the Jews were responsible for starting both world wars.

Historians of course have the right to question the veracity of any historical event, but the prevailing opinion among historians is that the claims of the Holocaust deniers are both false and offensive. Not only have they ignored volumes of evidence from the Nuremberg Trials, but their actions have often been calculatedly offensive, the *Journal of Historical Review*, for example, offering $80,000 in 1980 for proof that a single Jew was gassed by the Nazis and $25,000 for a bar of soap made from Jewish body fat.

Holocaust denial in Europe

Right-wing American extremists who denied the existence of the Holocaust also had their counterparts in Europe. One of the most influential of these was the Frenchman Paul Rassinier, the author of five books, the best known of which was *Debunking the genocide myth*.[5] During the 1960s, Rassinier, who had some influence on H. Elmer Barnes, was the first to question the actual existence of the gas chambers. His fellow countryman, Robert Faurrison, a former literature lecturer, argued in his *Testimony for the defence* that Anne Frank's diary was a forgery and that the gas chambers were an 'enormous hoax'. (Anne Frank's diary, a seminal Holocaust text, has often been a target for Holocaust deniers.)

In Britain, the best-known revisionist is David Irving. As well as claiming (unconvincingly, in the view of most historians) that Hitler was the weakest German leader of the twentieth century, Irving went on to claim that Hitler knew nothing about the Holocaust. His statement, for example, that 'Heydrich had not in fact secured Hitler's approval for liquidating the Jews'[6] is typical of several that try to exculpate Hitler from responsibility for the Holocaust. The absence of a single document signed by Hitler authorising the mass murder of the Jews does not exonerate Hitler from responsibility for the Holocaust, and it must be remembered that his laziness in bureaucratic matters meant that his orders to his subordinates were often given orally. Why Irving wished to shift the responsibility for the Holocaust from Hitler to Himmler and Heydrich is unclear; perhaps the reason is that, in order for Hitler to remain an icon of the neo-fascists, the revisionists feel that his association with the Holocaust has to be disproved.

Other British contributors to the Holocaust-denial genre cannot claim to have written serious historical works (as, perhaps, Irving can); for the most part they are a ragbag collection of former members of the neo-fascist National Front and British Movement. Germany, too, has produced Holocaust deniers, who typically hardly qualify for the more respectable title of 'revisionists', given their rejection of normal historical-research methodology. Perhaps more significant in its implications was the rise in support for Nazi-style politics in the former East Germany following Germany's reunification in 1990.

The significance of the Holocaust denial

The techniques used by Holocaust deniers are regarded as an affront to professional historians because they distort documentary evidence or involve outright fabrication of evidence. More importantly, however, they are an affront to the survivors of the Holocaust: to have lived through the horrors of Auschwitz and then to have the reality of your suffering denied adds insult to terrible injury, to say the least. Yet in democratic societies the right to raise difficult questions about the past (including the Holocaust) is implicit in their natures, however offensive such questions may be (it should be noted, though, that in Germany Holocaust denial is a criminal offence). Only when a clear incitement to racial hatred appears in publications can legislation be invoked against the offenders. Such incitement has indeed occurred as a result of the close link between neo-fascist movements in the post-war world and Holocaust denial. It is no accident that the American self-styled 'Nazi' leader George Lincoln Rockwell claimed that the Holocaust was a 'monstrous and profitable fraud', or that the leader of the French *Front national*, Jean-Marie Le Pen, said that the number of Holocaust victims had been exaggerated. Such political leaders are, perhaps, bound to make such claims in order to try to distance themselves and their movements from the worst crime of fascism in history, the Holocaust.

The duty of maintaining objectivity and vigilance when dealing with such forms of 'pseudo-history' as the Holocaust denial and revisionism remains. This is why the study of the Holocaust is so important. Until the 1960s, the Holocaust attracted little attention from historians, perhaps because it was such an appalling and difficult phenomenon to study. Today, however, the historical debate about the Holocaust is part of a much larger argument about genocide and racism in the twentieth century. But it is nevertheless conducted within the parameters of normal academic debate and not within the boundaries set by pseudo-academic, anti-Semitic fanatics like Barnes, Butz and Faurrison.

Document case study

The Holocaust deniers

7.1 The impact of First World War atrocity stories in the USA

Twenty years later, when reports reached Americans about Nazi Germany's use of gas to kill Jews, the lingering impact of these false atrocity tales was evident. Americans dismissed the second spate of stories as yet another set of tall tales about the Germans. The problem, of course, was that this time the stories were true.

Source: D. Lipstadt, *Denying the Holocaust*, London, 1994, p. 34

7.2 Barnes on the gas chambers

The courageous author [Rassinier] lays the chief blame for misrepresentation on those whom we must call the swindlers of the crematoria, the Israeli politicians who derive billions of marks from non-existent, mythical and imaginary cadavers, whose numbers have been reckoned in an unusually distorted and dishonest manner.

Source: H. Elmer Barnes, 'Zionist fraud', in *American Mercury*, 1968

7.3 An attack on the Institute for Historical Review

This Institute, camouflaged as a scholarly institution, took on the task of denying the historicity of the Holocaust. Using the talents of anti-Semitic writers with far-out notions of historical reality, many of them from abroad, the Institute in 1979 launched the first of a series of annual pseudo-scholarly meetings that were parodies of bona fide academic conferences.

Source: L. Dawidowicz, *The war against the Jews, 1933–45*, London, 1975, p. xxi

7.4 An attack on the Holocaust deniers

Amazingly, considering the volume of documentary evidence to the contrary, an ever increasing number of authors is joining forces to claim that the Holocaust was a Jewish swindle to enrich themselves and, since 1948, to justify the Jewish state at the expense of the Palestinians; that prisoners at the Nuremberg Trials were tortured to obtain confessions; that the Allied bombings were just as bad as the alleged German atrocities; and that the Zyklon B gas was only used in the concentration camps as an insecticide or to curb typhus.

Source: E. Marriott, *Evening Standard*, 5 September 1996

7.5 Should the deniers be taken seriously?

Jean-Claude Pressac's 'Truth Prevails: Demolishing Holocaust Denial', which showed that the Auschwitz gas chambers were destroyed and then reconstituted by the communists after the war as a warning and a monument. There was, apparently, no trace of gas in the concrete and the reconstruction was, in detail, inaccurate. This does not mean that the gas chambers did not exist, and Pressac is not one of those crazy 'revisionists' (are these people really worth the fuss?).

Source: Norman Stone, *Sunday Times*, 12 July 1998

Document case-study questions

1 What light does 7.1 throw on the reasons why some Americans found the Holocaust denial plausible?

2 In what ways does 7.2 make it clear that H. Elmer Barnes is a Holocaust denier?

3 Explain what you understand by the phrases the 'historicity of the Holocaust', 'far-out notions of historical reality' and 'pseudo-scholarly meetings' contained in 7.3.

4 What examples does 7.4 give of a) relativism and b) Holocaust denial?

5 Compare and contrast the statements made by the writers in 7.4 and 7.5. Is the rejection of Holocaust-denial propaganda 'really worth the fuss', as Stone asks in 7.5? Justify your answer.

Notes and references

1 H. Elmer Barnes, 'Revisionism. A key to peace', *Rampart Journal* (1966), quoted in L. Dawidowicz, 'Lies about the Holocaust', *Commentary 70* (1980).

2 D. Lipstadt, *Denying the Holocaust*, London, 1994, p. 80.

3 A. R. Butz, *The hoax of the twentieth century*, Torrance, 1977.

4 L. Dawidowicz, *The war against the Jews, 1933–45*, London, 1975, p. xxi.

5 P. Rassinier, *Debunking the genocide myth*, Torrance, 1978.

6 D. Irving, *Hitler's war*, London, 1977, p. 15.

East and west: collaboration and the Holocaust experience

Nazi racist ideology decreed that there would be a distinct difference between the way in which the Nazis behaved in western Europe and in eastern Europe. The Slavs which populated eastern Europe were regarded by the Nazis as *Untermenschen* ('subhumans') and were consequently deemed fit only to be slave labourers, whereas the peoples of western Europe were considered to be 'superior racial types'. The further east the Nazis moved on the continent of Europe, the more inhuman their behaviour to the people who fell into their hands became. Their attitude towards groups like Jews, Gypsies, black people, the mentally and physically disabled and homosexuals was, however, consistent in its intolerance and murderous nature. Numerically, of course, the Jews, whom the Nazis considered to be the primary 'enemies' of their regime, suffered the most.

The experience of Jews in western Europe

The Jewish experience in western Europe was somewhat different to that of those in eastern Europe for a number of reasons. The Nazis acted more slowly against them following the German military victories in the west in 1940 than they had done against Jews in Poland or would do in the USSR. This was partly because rival agencies within the Nazi regime, like the Foreign Office and the military, were reluctant to give total control of Jewish policy to the SS, as had happened in the east, and because the Nazis believed that the people of western Europe were of a higher 'racial order'. The SS's Reich Security Head Office (RSHA), under Heydrich, was still the single most important agency for Jewish policy in the west, but it was not omnipotent.

The Nazis also suffered from a lack of manpower in the west and were thus more reliant on local fascists (like the Belgian Rexists), bureaucrats and police forces to assist them. Another significant factor which determined the Nazis' policies towards the Jews in western Europe was that Jews were more broadly dispersed than in the east and were usually also more closely integrated into wider society (as in Germany itself), which meant that sealed-off ghettos were not created in western Europe. Western European Jews were fewer in number than in eastern Europe and could thus more easily be assembled at railheads before being sent to the death camps. Finally, before the Nazis took decisive action against them between 1942 and 1943, western European Jews were encouraged to emigrate; their property was sometimes confiscated, but the Nazis had other priorities in the early days of the occupation of their countries.

Yugoslavia

By contrast with Jews in western Europe, those in Yugoslavia, who were living outside the main eastern European area of Jewish settlement, were treated savagely. The impetus for their vicious persecution by the Nazis seems to have been provided by an abortive communist revolt against the Germans in June 1941, two months after the Italian–German invasion of Yugoslavia. The revolt provided the *Wehrmacht* (the German army) with an excuse to take reprisals, and Jews and Gypsies, who were, in Nazi eyes, natural 'enemies' of the Third Reich, were easy targets. Lucy Dawidowicz notes how the German forces were 'embarrassingly efficient'[1] at rounding up Jews for slaughter in Semlin, Serbia, at a time when mass-gassing techniques were not yet available to the Nazis.

It is important to note the involvement of the *Wehrmacht* in the rounding-up of the Jews. The order for reprisals against the Jews came not from Hitler or Himmler directly, but from Wilhelm Keitel, the representative in Berlin of the OKW (*Oberkommando der Wehrmacht*), the army's high command. There had been some instances of high-ranking German officers objecting to the slaughter of Jews in Poland in 1939, but there were no such objections on the part of *Wehrmacht* officers in Yugoslavia, or in the USSR after June 1941. Indeed, the *Wehrmacht* seems to have been only too enthusiastic in its co-operation with the Nazi regime in the mass killings of Jews and Soviets alike. The expansion of a programme which had been designed in the first instance to annihilate communists appears to have presented no problem to the *Wehrmacht*'s generals when it was extended to the Jews. The argument that German army units were inherently more 'decent' than the SS therefore cannot be sustained.

Collaboration with the Nazis

The subject of collaboration with the Nazis in occupied Europe during the Second World War is a painful and controversial one, particularly when such collaboration involved collusion with the Nazis in the murder of the Jews. The Nazi preference for using local authorities and police to round up Jews in the west has already been noted. Nowhere did the Nazis find more willing accomplices than in Vichy France.

The Vichy regime and the Jews

The German defeat of France in 1940 can be said to have given French anti-Semites and racists an opportunity to act against French Jews. Far from having been bullied by the Nazis into adopting anti-Semitic policies, the Vichy regime (which was named after the town where it was based) under Marshal Philippe Pétain actively co-operated with the Nazis and, indeed, formulated its own anti-Jewish legislation.

The regime's so-called 'National Revolution' involved the promulgation of anti-Jewish laws only three months after the Vichy government was established in June 1940. Under the *Statuts des Juifs* ('Jewish Statutes'), anyone who had three Jewish grandparents was defined as 'Jewish'; anyone who had a Jewish spouse and two Jewish grandparents was similarly categorised. Jews were excluded from the French army's officer corps, the judiciary, teaching, all elected offices and the press. The assets of wealthy Jewish families, like the Rothschilds, were also seized. Jews were furthermore deprived of their French citizenship. (Pétain, although an anti-Semite, had commanded the French army during the First World War and excluded Jews who had honourable war records from the provisions of the legislation.) Those Jews who could fled from the clutches of the Vichy regime into the Italian zone of occupation in the south of France where, they hoped, their safety would be assured. In a sense, the anti-Dreyfusards of the 1890s (see Chapter 1) can be said to have triumphed in 1940.

Part of France, the occupied zone, remained under direct German rule. Here, too, there was clear evidence of French anti-Semitism: French policemen, for example, co-operated with the Nazis in the rounding-up of Jews, who were then sent to the notorious Drancy holding centre in Paris. From Drancy, they subsequently went to their deaths in Auschwitz and elsewhere in 1942. The available figures suggest that 42,000 Jews, 6,000 of them children, were sent to Auschwitz alone, and one estimate suggests that as many as 76,000 Jews, a quarter of France's Jewish population, died in the death camps. While it is true that this last figure represents a lower percentage of deaths than those of Jews in other countries, like Belgium and The Netherlands, 'what remains particularly shameful was the extent to which the French authorities colluded with the Occupier in rounding up victims among the foreign Jews who had fled to France as refugees'.[2]

The French tendency for collusion with the Nazis mirrored what happened elsewhere in Europe, the deportation of foreign Jewish refugees arousing no protest, while that of local, well-integrated Jews did. As far as French political leaders, like the prime minister from 1942 to 1944, Pierre Laval, were concerned, foreign Jews were expendable as part of their efforts to do advantageous deals with the Nazis and even the French citizens within the Jewish community were deported. Members of the *Milice*, the Vichy regime's police force, proved themselves as ranking among the most vicious anti-Semites in Europe and were active in the hunt for Jews who had gone underground in the unoccupied zone. Many Jews joined the French Resistance against the German occupation.

The actions of the Vichy regime can be said to have besmirched France's libertarian and humanistic tradition. Any attempt to defend the Vichy regime by arguing that the situation would have been worse under a complete German occupation (which actually happened at the end of 1942) cannot be justified. Far from restoring French honour, as Pétain claimed, the Vichy regime represented the worst and most reactionary aspects of French society.

Denmark and Italy

There were two major exceptions to the depressing picture of anti-Semitic collusion with the Nazis in occupied Europe during the Second World War. One was Denmark, from which almost all the indigenous population of 8,000 Jews, most of whom lived in Copenhagen, were smuggled safely across the sea to neutral Sweden. The Danish king, Christian X, ostentatiously wore the Star of David himself, thereby openly showing his opposition to the Nazis' persecution of the Jews. Only 400 Danish Jews perished in the death camps.

Although Italy was ostensibly an ally of Germany, with which it had signed the 'Pact of Steel' in 1939, most Italians never made any serious attempt to co-operate with the Nazis in the implementation of the 'Final Solution', despite the attempt of the Italian leader, Mussolini, to copy his fellow fascist dictator, Hitler, by introducing anti-Semitic legislation in 1938.

Wherever Italian forces were involved in the occupation of other European countries – as in Greece, Yugoslavia, France or Albania – they protected rather than persecuted Jews. Perhaps surprisingly, the Germans made little apparent effort to force them to hand over Jews; whether this was a result of Hitler's respect for Mussolini or because only a relatively small number of Jews were involved remains uncertain. In contrast with the controversy surrounding the behaviour of Pope Pius XII in not condemning the Nazis' persecution of the Jews (see Chapter 6), his predecessor, Pius XI, had condemned Mussolini's anti-Semitic legislation in 1938, a fact which tends to be forgotten when the overall record of the Catholic Church with regard to the Holocaust is considered.

For his part, Mussolini was not a convinced racist, as Hitler was, but he did nothing to prevent the deportation of thousands of Italian Jews to death camps by the Germans, thus colluding with Hitler's racist policies. The Italian Fascist troops were furthermore clearly guilty of barbarous and racist practices in Abyssinia (Ethiopia) between 1935 and 1936, following their invasion of the country, and in Yugoslavia between 1941 and 1943. Although the Italian forces can be said to have deserved credit for their protection of Jews, this fact should be remembered.

More general points have also been made about the fate of Italian and Danish Jews. In both countries Jews were not only relatively few in number but were also well integrated into wider society. They were therefore not perceived as presenting any kind of internal threat to these countries as they were in the eastern European states, which had much larger Jewish populations, for example. Neither had there been a large influx of foreign Jewish refugees into Denmark and Italy, as there had been into Belgium and France, for instance.

Central and eastern Europe

After 1941 there were two categories of state in eastern Europe:

1 those, like Croatia and Slovakia, which were Nazi puppet states and depended on German support for their existence; and
2 older nation states, such as Romania, Hungary and Bulgaria, which were reluctant German allies and were ultimately occupied by German forces.

Croatia was the first area in occupied Europe to be declared *judenfrei* ('Jew free') in 1942. From 1941 to 1945 it was ruled, with German support, by the fascist dictator Ante Pavelić, who was responsible for the mass murder of some 200,000 Serbs in concentration camps.

Slovakia, which had been detached from Czechoslovakia in 1938, was ruled by the Catholic cleric Josef Tiso from 1939 to 1945 and provided the first victims for the Auschwitz gas ovens in 1942. Slovak Jews were also forced to build the first crematoria at Auschwitz, where they, along with Czechoslovakian Jews, were subsequently gassed.

In the other eastern European states (Poland apart, which was under direct Nazi control) their governments had a degree of control over the extent of anti-Semitic persecution. In Bulgaria, for example, 50,000 Jews survived as a result of the public protests of King Boris III (who ruled until 1943) and the Orthodox Church against the Germans' deportation plans; by the spring of 1943 the Germans had abandoned their efforts to deport Bulgarian Jews to the death camps. Remarkably, there were more Jews alive in Bulgaria in 1945 than there had been in 1939.

Romania had its own fascist organisation, the Iron Guard, which was heavily involved in anti-Semitic excesses, specifically targeting Jews who had lived in Soviet-occupied Bessarabia (a Romanian province until 1940). The Jews were accused of having co-operated with the Soviet occupiers and were deported to the death camps by the Romanian authorities. Many Jews in other parts of Romania escaped, but when the Nazis occupied Hungary in 1944 they deported Jews living in the Romanian-governed part of Transylvania (much of Transylvania had been ceded to Romania by Hungary in 1940).

Hungary had passed anti-Semitic legislation under its dictator Miklós Horthy, but it had been laxly applied. Until the German occupation, Jews were not required to wear the Star of David and so-called 'straw men' were used to protect Jewish-owned businesses and estates (on payment of a large sum of money, Christians acted as the nominal owners of Jewish properties, while the Jews retained real control of them). The Hungarian Jews' situation changed in 1944, however, when the Germans' direct occupation of the country (as described in Chapter 5) heralded the end of the Hungarian Jewish community.

The role of Horthy in the fate of the Hungarian Jews is controversial. His critics argue that he preferred a German to a Soviet occupation, even though inherent in this was the genocide of the Hungarian Jews. Yet Horthy had already condoned the existence of the anti-Semitic Arrow Cross Party, which was active in the mass murder of Hungarian Jews between 1944 and 1945. In October 1944, after Horthy had stopped the deportations of Jews in response to global outrage, the Nazis replaced him with an Arrow Cross government under Ferenc Szálasi. Szálasi's government was no more than a German puppet regime and resumed the deportations of Jews.

The vicious nature of anti-Semitic violence in eastern Europe (Romania had a particularly bad tradition of anti-Semitism) was underlined by the massacres of Jews carried out by Hungarian and Romanian soldiers. Both states sent troops to fight against communism in the USSR alongside the German forces. Romanian troops were responsible for the massacre of 26,000 Jews in Odessa in 1941 and for the drowning of others in the river Dniester in the same year. Hungarian soldiers participated in the mass killings of Jews in 1941 and 1942, forcing other Jews to join labour battalions and then working them to death.

Poland

Poland was a case apart among the eastern European states. Like Romania, it, too, had a bad record of anti-Semitism during the inter-war period. It also had the largest Jewish population (3 million) of any European state in 1939. After the Nazi conquest of the country in September 1939, with the help of the USSR, which invaded from the east in accordance with the terms of the Nazi–Soviet Pact (1939), Poland disappeared as an independent state. There was therefore no Polish collaborationist regime and, indeed, instances of collaboration with the Nazis in Poland were virtually non-existent. In part, at least, this was the result of the Nazis' unwillingness to become involved in any form of co-operation with people whom they regarded as being 'subhuman'. The Poles, in Nazi eyes, had also made the mistake of daring to resist Germany's invasion of their country by force and would subsequently be made to pay for their temerity. The first task that the Nazis set themselves in Poland was the elimination of Polish intellectuals and potential political leaders who might have provided a threat to them. Ultimately, 3 million Poles died alongside the 3 million Polish Jews; about half the population of the Polish capital, Warsaw – both Jewish and Polish – died between 1939 and 1945.

The German administration of Poland reflected the Nazis' racial and ideological imperatives. Between 1939 and June 1941, when the Germans invaded the Soviet zone of Poland, the country was divided into two. The western provinces were directly annexed by the Third Reich and were subjected to a ruthless policy of 'Germanisation'. Ethnic Germans were given Polish land, while Poles were subjected to 'ethnic screening' in order for the Nazis to ascertain whether they had any 'unacceptable racial characteristics'. All the other areas of German-occupied Poland were placed within the so-called 'General Government', under SS and military rule. From late 1939, it was into the General Government area that Jews were forced to move, as sealed-off ghettos were established for them. Jewish councils, supported by Jewish policemen, then ran the ghettos under overall Nazi control.

When the Germans over-ran the Soviet-occupied part of Poland in June 1941 the number of Jews taken captive increased, as did the number of ghettos. The Germans also invaded the Soviet-controlled Baltic republics of Lithuania, Latvia and Estonia in 1941, the republics' Jewish populations thus also falling into Nazi hands. It was Poland, however, which remained the focus of the Nazis' racist policies, and which bore the brunt of the Nazis' 'ethnic-cleansing' programme, which reached its peak between 1941 and 1945. The anti-Semitic policies of the pre-war Polish governments paled in significance in comparison with the Nazis' anti-Jewish onslaught.

Collaboration and the Holocaust

8.1 Local reactions to the deportation of Jews

Yet in France and elsewhere in the west, trouble arose when it came to shipping western European natives off to some 'unknown destination'. Historians have noted how, in 1943, when foreign Jews could no longer be found so easily to fill the deportation quotas, even former collaborationist officials began to drag their feet. Across western Europe, the local engines of support for deportation began to misfire. Police forces in France and the Netherlands began to lose their taste for rounding up Jews once the manhunts turned to local citizens in addition to outsiders.

Source: M. Marrus, *The Holocaust in history*, London, 1987, p. 72

8.2 Collaboration in Vichy France

Institutional anti-Semitism was made easier by general indifference. Only Jewish and Christian welfare organisations or international humanitarians protested against the enforced internment in appalling conditions of about 40,000 foreign Jews living in the Free Zone, the Vichy-administered area left unoccupied by the German army in the first years of the war. Nor was there any public outcry when at least 3,000 internees died of starvation, disease and maltreatment during the first two winters.

Source: P. Webster, *Pétain's crime. The full story of French collaboration in the Holocaust*, London, 1990, p. 5

8.3 Anti-Semitism in Italy

He [Mussolini] continued to assert that possession of an East African Empire was what forced him to bring these racial questions into the open, yet the charter made it abundantly clear that not just Arabs and Ethiopians, but Jews too were an inferior race. As with the goose step, he was again anxious to insist that he was not copying anyone else; on the contrary he said he had himself been a consistent racist for the last fifteen years.

It had to be admitted, however, that despite the usual unanimous vote of approval in parliament, the new racial policy was not well received by the public. Italians were therefore told that they must learn to feel like a master race and suppress any sense of pity for the persecuted.

Source: D. Mack Smith, *Mussolini*, London, 1981, pp. 221–22

8.4 The process of ghettoisation in eastern Europe

Concentration was followed by segregation and isolation. The 160,000 Jews crammed into Lodz were formally sealed off from the rest of the town in May 1940 to form the first ghetto in Nazi-dominated eastern Europe. By November of the same year, a high brick wall sealed close to half a million Jews into the Warsaw ghetto. With the walls came the cutting of telephone lines, whilst postal services were at the mercy of the Gestapo who would accept letters written only in German or Polish, not in Yiddish. Only the smaller ghettos remained unsealed.

Source: E. Crampton, *Eastern Europe in the twentieth century*, London, 1994, p. 185

8.5 The co-operation of Nazi agencies in the Holocaust

Civil servants, from the heads of major government departments down to the small fry organising the timetabling of deportation trains, worked hard to turn ideological irrationality into bureaucratic regulations for discrimination. The army, unhappy at some of the 'excesses' in Poland, were co-operative in the fight against the 'Jewish-Bolshevik' arch-enemy. And in the SS, Hitler had the most dynamic organisation in the Third Reich, drawing its entire ethos from a doctrine of racial dominance and wedded to the centrality of the need to solve the 'Jewish Question'. German genocide therefore, was far from one man's doing.

Source: I. Kershaw, *Hitler*, London, 1991, p. 158

Document case-study questions

1 What does 8.1 suggest was the basis for objections to the deportation of domestic, as apart opposed to foreign, Jews in western Europe?

2 Use the material in 8.2 and what you have read in this chapter to explain the hostility towards Jews in Vichy France.

3 What does 8.3 suggest was the basis for Mussolini's anti-Semitic policy? Explain why it was unsuccessful.

4 Use 8.4 and what you have read in this chapter and in Chapter 5 to explain the significance of the process of ghettoisation. What was the purpose of the Gestapo policy of accepting 'letters written only in German or Polish'?

5 What does 8.5 tell historians about the respective roles of the German civil service, the army and the SS in the Holocaust? How much was the Holocaust in Europe a result of German initiatives or local willingness to co-operate with them? Justify your answer.

Notes and references

1 L. Dawidowicz, *The war against the Jews, 1933–45*, London, 1975, p. 176.

2 J. MacMillan, *Twentieth-century France*, London, 1992, p. 138.

The legacy of the Holocaust

The Holocaust is regarded by many historians as the single most horrific event of the twentieth century. Its shadow lay over the immediate post-war period and its legacy remains with us today. The immediate problem facing the Allies in the aftermath of the Second World War was how to punish those who had planned and implemented the genocide of the Jews. Another problem was the issue of compensation for the victims – if, indeed, any level of compensation could be adequate for the appalling experiences which had been inflicted on the survivors of the Holocaust. A third issue arising from the Holocaust was focused on the inception of the Jewish state of Israel in 1948 and how the Holocaust experience affected its relations with the outside world. Finally, there is the question of what lessons can be learnt from the Holocaust, both in terms of institutionalised racism and inter-state relations.

Crime and punishment

Six million Jews are estimated to have died as a consequence of the Holocaust, both inside and outside the death camps. Hundreds of thousands of Gypsies, homosexuals, black people, the mentally and physically disabled and those belonging to other minority groups also perished. The Allied powers eventually reached an agreement that the surviving Nazi leaders should be charged with crimes against humanity at Nuremberg, in Germany, in trials that lasted from 1945 to 1946. Many volumes of evidence were accumulated against Nazi leaders like Himmler and Heydrich (neither of whom actually faced trial, Himmler having committed suicide in 1945 following his capture by British troops and Heydrich having been assassinated by Czech nationalists in Prague in 1942) and their underlings, who had carried out the mass murders.

The Nuremberg Trials were predominantly concerned with bringing the main Nazi leaders to trial if they were still alive. (By the time that the International Military Tribunal met at Nuremberg in 1945 Hitler, Goebbels and Himmler had all already committed suicide and Göring would do the same before his sentence of death by hanging could be carried out.)

Despite some attempts by Nazi apologists to portray the Nuremberg Trials as show trials, they were, in fact, 'remarkably calm and dispassionate',[1] although there was some haggling among the Allies about appropriate punishments for those on trial (the Soviets wanted to execute all the defendants). But in the end 10 Nazi leaders were hanged, all having been proved to have been implicated in

The final session at the Nuremberg War Trials, 1 October 1946. On the front row, left to right: Göring (committed suicide after being sentenced to death), Hess (life sentence), Ribbentrop (hanged), Keitel (hanged), Kaltenbrunner (hanged), Rosenberg (hanged), Frank (hanged), Frick (hanged), Streicher (hanged), Funk (life sentence), Schacht (life sentence). On the back row: Dönitz (life sentence), Raeder (life sentence), Schirach (imprisoned), Sauckel (hanged), Jodl (hanged), von Papen (acquitted), Seyss-Inquart (hanged), Speer (life sentence), von Neurath (imprisoned), Fritzsche (acquitted).

crimes of genocide. The tribunal was neither deceived by the plea of *Wehrmacht* leaders, like Wilhelm Keitel and Alfred Jodl, that they had merely been doing their duty as soldiers and knew nothing about the 'Final Solution', nor by the general excuse that the defendants did not know about the reality of the Holocaust, which, they said, was Hitler's, and not their fault.

Was justice done at Nuremberg? Probably not entirely, because many leading Nazis escaped punishment (Eichmann, for example, fled to Argentina). But it must be remembered that the task facing the Allied powers was a truly daunting one. Eight million people had joined the Nazi Party and in the face of such numbers the Americans soon abandoned the concept of the Germans' 'collective responsibility' for the Holocaust (a concept that has been subsequently applied by the historian Daniel Goldhagen[2]) which they had originally favoured. The Nuremberg Trials dealt with the Nazi leadership, although the selection procedure for the defendants was imperfect (some minor figures should probably not have been put on trial at all).

De-Nazification

The Allied powers were determined to purge Germany of the influence of national socialism. Other trials followed those at Nuremberg, like that of Hoess, the commandant at Auschwitz, who was deeply implicated in the genocide of the Jews. Despite the efforts of the Allied forces, who deliberately made the German inhabitants of towns like Weimar, which was close to Buchenwald, bury the emaciated corpses of the Nazis' victims in the immediate aftermath of the Second World War, too many Germans were unwilling to face the reality and implications of the Nazis' crimes. The real horror of the extermination camps, as the historian Walter Laqueur[3] has pointed out, was only really brought home to the German public when people like Hoess were tried during the late 1950s.

It has been suggested that for younger Germans the trial of Adolf Eichmann in 1961 marked a watershed in their view of their country's history. Eichmann had escaped to Argentina after the war (he was one of several SS killers who fled to Latin America), where he was subsequently kidnapped by the Israeli secret service, Mossad. Eichmann was then brought to Israel, tried in Jerusalem, found guilty of war crimes and finally executed in 1962. As a result of Eichmann's trial, a younger generation of Germans than those who had lived under the Third Reich refused to accept the often-given excuse that resistance to totalitarianism was impossible or that atrocities were inevitable during wartime. Yet a large number of former Nazis were still lodged in the West German administration (including a federal president, Heinrich Lübke) well into the 1960s.

One significant factor that contributed to the disinclination of the Allied powers to continue the process of retribution against Nazi war criminals was undoubtedly the Cold War. By the late 1940s relations between the USSR and the Western powers were already very poor, and the USA in particular wanted West Germany, which comprised the three Western powers' – the USA, Britain and France – zones of occupation, as an ally (East Germany was under Soviet control). The Western Allies were unwilling to devote resources to tracking down any surviving war criminals when a war with the USSR seemed a distinct possibility between 1948 and 1949 and, indeed, thereafter.

The responsibility for trying war criminals was therefore turned over to the West German and East German governments. The latter, perhaps unsurprisingly, given its strong communist, anti-fascist dynamic, was more zealous in its pursuit of Nazi war criminals, but it refused to see itself as the 'heir' of the Third Reich, branding crimes committed between 1933 and 1945 the responsibility of the 'fascists'. West Germany, however, made an honourable effort to maintain such prosecutions, in a way, for example, that has never been evident in Japan. Nevertheless, by the mid-1960s thousands of cases remained unresolved and the prosecution period had to be extended beyond 1965, the original time limit set for prosecutions. The West German government's efforts to protect a youthful generation from the impact of Nazi racism and propaganda were partly successful, although 'Hitler's children', the leftist radicals of the 1960s, many of whom had been born under the Third Reich, reacted fiercely to what they perceived to be the authoritarianism of the West German state.

Compensation

Ranged alongside the issue of the punishment of Nazi war criminals was the question of compensating the victims of Nazi crimes. In this instance, the federal German chancellor from 1949 to 1963, Konrad Adenauer, was responsible in 1953 for introducing a law which provided for compensation to be made to Israel, as well as to individual Jews who had been the victims of Nazi anti-Semitism. Israel received West German loans totalling $715 million (about £1,190 million) between 1953 and 1965. By contrast, East Germany, having refused to assume responsibility for any of the crimes of the fascist era before 1945, made no such gesture.

Other states, too, proved less willing than West Germany to acknowledge that the survivors of the Holocaust deserved justice. One such offender was Switzerland, which had profited from its neutrality during the Second World War by acting as a repository of the gold stolen from the Jews by the Nazis as part of the Holocaust process. (Some of this gold had been extracted from the teeth of death-camp victims before being melted down and formed into gold bars, which were then deposited in Swiss bank vaults.) The Swiss, whose banking laws are strict, proved extremely resistant to responding to calls that they should give up their ill-gotten gains. Elaborately worded excuses were made to the relatives of Holocaust victims who had deposited funds in Switzerland when they wanted to gain access to the accounts.

Ultimately, after following a strategy of obfuscation and delaying tactics from 1947, the Swiss were forced in 1997 to set up a compensation fund equivalent to $2.9 billion (about £1.7 billion), which would produce an annual figure of 350 million Swiss francs (about £8.75 million) with which to compensate the victims of both the Holocaust and of all human catastrophes. It was officially admitted that there had been 'moral lapses' in the Swiss government's policy during the Second World War, although the wide brief given to the compensation fund seemed to some people to have been an attempt to evade making a full acknowledgement of Swiss guilt. Pressure from the World Jewish Congress and the US government, together with expensive law suits brought by the relatives of Holocaust victims against Swiss banks pending in the USA, undoubtedly forced the Swiss into making these concessions.

The Swiss banks were not the only ones who were unwilling to grant access to the accounts of Holocaust victims. In 1998, for example, relatives of Holocaust victims who had deposited money in British banks also had had difficulty in extracting funds from the accounts, being rebutted by claims that their relatives had been 'enemy aliens' during the Second World War. Such extraordinary bureaucratic insensitivity to this issue on the part of banking houses has been a feature of the post-war period.

A similar insensitivity also prevailed at official state levels. In July 1998, for instance, it was announced that 500 surviving Jewish victims of Nazi persecution would obtain just £400 each from a £1 million fund set up by the Foreign Office in London. Such levels of compensation seem miserly, even if a fund totalling £37 million was subsequently set up as the result of an international conference on looted Nazi gold held in December 1997. As was the case before 1939, when the issue was that of Jewish refugees rather than of compensation, it always seemed to be someone else's problem. It was, at least, a positive feature of British policy in 1998 that it was announced that around £600,000 would be paid to an estimated 70,000 Holocaust survivors living in the former Soviet republics of the Ukraine, Byelorussia, Russia and Moldova. Furthermore, in December 1998 the British government announced that £25 million would be made available to the relatives of Jews whose accounts had been frozen because they lived in enemy states during the Second World War.

Israel and the Holocaust

The Holocaust has been one of the most profound influences on the Jewish state of Israel, which was set up in 1948 when the Holocaust was already over.

The Holocaust's initial impact was to leave hundreds of thousands of death-camp survivors adrift in central and eastern Europe. Understandably, most of them looked to Palestine, where Jews had what may be termed a 'national home' after 1917, as a potential refuge. Very few wished to return to their original homelands of Germany, Austria or Poland, where they had witnessed and experienced such terrible events, and so the Jewish populations in these countries never recovered to reach anything like their pre-war levels.

The foundation of Israel

The situation regarding the proposed foundation of a Jewish state in the immediate post-war period was complex. Britain, the colonial power in Palestine, was against the idea of the creation of a Jewish state there. (The British had, in fact, banned Jewish immigration into Palestine in 1944 as a reaction to the hostility of local Arabs to such a migration.) The Foreign Office was pro-Arab and unsympathetic to the plight of the displaced Jews. This attitude did not change when the Labour politician Ernest Bevin replaced the Conservative Anthony Eden as foreign secretary in 1945. Regardless of the fact that so many death-camp survivors wanted to go to Palestine, the British refused to change their policy, even though it made Britain highly unpopular abroad, especially in the United States.

Terror and counter-terror

The Jewish reaction was twofold:

1 inside Palestine, Jewish settlers set up Irgun and the 'Stern Gang' (as the British called the *Lohamei Herut Israel Lehi*, the 'Fighters for the Freedom of Israel'), two organisations which used terror tactics against the British forces in Palestine;
2 outside Palestine, Zionist groups organised attempts to send death-camp survivors to Palestine illegally.

The result was effectively a war between the Jewish freedom-fighters (or 'terrorists', as the British regarded them) and the British authorities. The British maintained a blockade to keep out the shiploads of Holocaust survivors who wanted to settle in Palestine, while Irgun and the Stern Gang attacked British troops. In July 1946 Irgun blew up the British military headquarters at the King David Hotel in Jerusalem, killing 91 people and injuring many more. The British retaliated by interrogating 120,000 Jews and arresting hundreds of them, but despite placing a reward of £2,000 on his head they failed to arrest the Irgun leader, Menachem Begin, who would become the prime minister of Israel from 1977 to 1983.

A year later, the British turned back 4,000 Holocaust survivors who had travelled to Palestine by sea in the *Exodus*. Only when the survivors refused to disembark in France, as the British had ordered, did the issue receive international recognition, but even then the unfortunate survivors were forced by the British to return to internment camps in Germany.

Meanwhile, the war between Irgun and the British had become even more vicious. When the British adopted a policy of caning captured 'terrorists' in 1947 Irgun responded by kidnapping and flogging a group of British soldiers, while the execution of three Irgun members led to the retaliatory murder of two British army sergeants by Irgun.

Anti-Semitic outbreaks in Britain

The news that the two sergeants had been murdered in Palestine led to an outbreak of anti-Semitic rioting in Britain. Jewish-owned shops were attacked in Lancashire and synagogues were defaced. In August 1947 in Liverpool, 80 men who worked in an abattoir refused to process meat intended for Jewish consumption; according to *The Times* newspaper, they then passed a resolution saying that their action would continue until 'organised terrorism in Palestine ceased and the leaders are given the same taste of British justice as the German gangsters in the war'.

Britain was not alone in experiencing anti-Semitic outbreaks so soon after the Holocaust. An anti-Jewish outrage, which was reminiscent of the pogroms of the Middle Ages, took place in Kielce, in Poland, in 1946, for example, which was made even more offensive by the region's close association with the Holocaust and the death camps. In this instance, a group of Soviet Jews, *en route* for Palestine, was attacked and murdered by local Poles, following the spreading of rumours about the Jews' alleged ritual murder of Catholic children.

An independent Israel emerges

Ultimately, in February 1947, the British government announced that it would give up its mandate over Palestine in May 1948. US public opinion had been outraged by the British policy in Palestine and financial pressures also meant that the British could no longer afford to keep an occupation force there; neither could the British prevent a series of tit-for-tat outrages between the Arabs and Jews. The whole problem of Palestine was now handed over to the United Nations Organisation (UN), which had been set up in 1945, to solve.

On 29 November 1947 the UN voted to partition Palestine into Jewish and Arab areas. This plan was accepted by David Ben-Gurion, the effective Jewish leader as chairman of the Jewish Agency, but was rejected by the Arabs. Thus when the British withdrew from Palestine on the agreed date of 14 May 1948 the Jews were attacked by the neighbouring Arab states of Syria, Transjordan and Egypt, which invaded Palestine. The Jews defended themselves successfully, but occupied land allocated by the UN to the Arabs. In 1947 there were some 900,000 Arabs in Palestine, but by the end of 1948 700,000 had fled as refugees to surrounding Arab states. A bitter legacy of hatred had been created in the region which survives to this day.

The Holocaust and Israel today

The memory of the Holocaust undoubtedly affected post-war Israeli policy, especially in the area of national security. Jews had been slaughtered in their millions by the Nazis yet this atrocity had evoked very little reaction from the outside world. Israel, it determined, would therefore take responsibility for its own preservation and would adopt the biblical policy of an 'eye for an eye and a tooth for a tooth'. This policy, while perhaps understandable, has created great difficulties in terms of creating harmonious Arab–Israeli relations.

In 1967, for example, Israel, which believed that it was about to be attacked by the Arab states, launched a pre-emptive strike against Jordanian and Egyptian military installations and won an overwhelming victory in the 'Six-day War', occupying part of Sinai, the West Bank, Old Jerusalem, the Golan Heights and the Gaza Strip. For years, the Israelis, defying a UN resolution, subsequently refused to return any of the territories that it had conquered in Egypt, Syria and Jordan. This refusal could perhaps have been justified on grounds of national security, but the triumph of Begin's Likud Party in the 1977 Israeli general election led to a much more intransigent attitude. Allied as it was to extremist Jewish groups, Likud advocated a provocative policy of imposing Jewish settlements on previously Arab-owned land. Given the tensions created by the absence of so many Palestinian Arabs, who had fled to neighbouring states, this policy made a difficult situation worse. From then on, the tolerant, largely secular culture of the original Jewish settlers was cast aside by Begin's successors as prime minister, Yitzhak Shamir during the 1980s and Binjamin Netanyahu during the 1990s. The promise of the 1993 Oslo Accord, whereby the Labour prime minister of Israel, Yitzhak Rabin, had agreed to return some territory to Palestinian control, was similarly not adhered to.

The deep wounds inflicted on the Israeli psyche by the Holocaust, together with Israel's claim on Jewish land that, it believes, has been its by right from biblical times, therefore created a deep division in Israeli society: religious Jews clashed with secular Jews. In 1995 a right-wing fanatic, Yigal Amir, shot dead Prime Minister Rabin, claiming afterwards that Rabin had betrayed the Jewish people by signing the Oslo Accords and giving away Jewish land and blaming the Palestinian Arabs for the crimes of the Nazis.

For their part, the Palestinians had turned to acts of terrorism during the 1960s and 1970s, motivated by their failure to regain their lost lands from Israel. Such acts of terrorism in turn placed an enormous national-security burden on Israel. The Israeli government of Netanyahu during the late 1990s seemed increasingly unwilling to make concessions to the Palestinian Arabs, under pressure from the ultra-Orthodox, right-wing Jewish movement to expand Israeli settlements in Arab-occupied land. Such right-wing Jews believe that the experience of the Holocaust, as well as a biblically based right, justifies Israel's territorial expansion and they often regard those who resist such Jewish claims as pro-Arab fascists or racists.

The non-Jewish world and the Holocaust

Their suffering in the Holocaust meant that after the Second World War the Jewish people were regarded with sympathy and goodwill, especially in the USA. In France, too, successive political leaders were influenced by the heroism of Jewish fighters in the French Resistance during the war and gave military support to the new Israeli state.

In practical terms, this sympathetic attitude ensured consistent US support for Israel, including massive amounts of financial aid and arms equipment. The Jewish lobby in the United States remains powerful and will also evoke the memory of the genocide of the Jews.

In contrast to the USA, until its demise in 1991 the other superpower, the USSR, was consistently hostile to Israel, apart from a brief period between 1947 and 1948. Indeed, why the USSR voted in favour of a Jewish state at the UN in 1947 is something of a mystery, for the Soviet Union had consistently opposed Zionism and in his later years the Soviet dictator, Josef Stalin (who died in 1953), was clearly anti-Semitic. It may be speculated that he may have supported Israel because of his enmity to British imperialism or that he saw Israel as a potential entry point for Soviet influence into the Middle East (Israel initially had a Labour government, which might have been an ally of the communist USSR).

Whatever its motives for supporting the establishment of the Jewish state, the USSR subsequently became a persistent opponent of Israel, providing arms to Israel's Arab enemies and pursuing a viciously anti-Semitic domestic policy during the 1970s and 1980s. Thousands of Soviet Jews were prevented from emigrating to Israel and persecuted if they campaigned on the issue. If ever any sympathy was felt for the victims of the Holocaust in the former Soviet Union state policy prevented it from being demonstrated.

The same was true of the official policy in the Soviet Union's communist satellite states. Rudolf Slansky, a Jewish communist leader in Czechoslovakia, was executed in 1951, for example, and there was a state-sponsored, anti-Semitic campaign in Poland during the 1970s. Jewish identity was something to be disguised if citizens wanted to advance themselves in communist countries, while Zionism was regarded as unacceptable precisely because it had stressed such a Jewish identity and had campaigned for a separate Jewish state since its foundation by Theodor Herzl (1866–1904) in the nineteenth century.

The Holocaust in memory

What impact does the Holocaust have on the contemporary world? There are obviously the physical reminders of the Holocaust, in the form of memorials in Tel Aviv, London and Washington, DC. There are the ghostly remnants of the camps themselves, at places like Auschwitz and Buchenwald. There are the constant reminders of the lack of adequate financial compensation of the victims of the Holocaust, while neo-fascist revivals across the globe attempt to deny or trivialise the event. It must be hoped that such reminders will ensure that the Holocaust will not be forgotten and that human rights and liberty will be defended in the future. For Jews, of course, the Holocaust will forever remain a painful, unforgettable memory.

It should not be forgotten that there have been other acts of genocide during the twentieth century. Little attention has been paid to the Ottoman Turks' genocidal policy towards the Armenians during the First World War, although the genocide of the 1970s in Cambodia has been well documented, both by film and literary sources, as have the most recent examples of 'ethnic cleansing' in Bosnia and Rwanda. Nevertheless, among all these instances of genocide it is likely that the systematic horror of the 'Final Solution' will remain paramount in popular memory, even as its survivors enter their seventies and eighties.

Could it happen again? The last word should surely be left to a Jew, Elie Wiesel.

Not that I foresee the possibility of Jews being massacred in the cities of America or in the forests of Europe [Wiesel wrote in 1968], but there is a certain climate, a certain mood in the making. As far as the Jewish people are concerned, the world has remained unchanged: as indifferent to our fate as its own.[4]

Indifference to racism, as much as racist prejudice itself, must always be guarded against. This necessity was confirmed by the creation of a UN-sponsored war-crimes court in July 1998, yet despite the legacy of the Holocaust it still took more than 50 years for the global community to achieve this.

Notes and references

1 A. and J. Tusa, *The Nuremberg Trial*, London, 1983, p. 490.

2 D. Goldhagen, *Hitler's willing executioners. Ordinary Germans and the Holocaust*, London, 1996.

3 W. Laqueur, *Europe in our time*, London, 1992, p. 26.

4 E. Wiesel, 'Ominous signs and unspeakable thoughts', in R. K. Chartock and J. Spencer (eds.), *Can it happen again? Chronicles of the Holocaust*, New York, 1995, p. 363.

Select bibliography

General surveys

There is now a large number of good, general texts about the Holocaust and anti-Semitism, including: M. Marrus, *The Holocaust in history*, London, 1987; L. Dawidowicz, *The war against the Jews, 1933–45*, London, 1975; P. Burrin, *Hitler and the Jews*, London, 1994; C. Browning, *The path to genocide*, Cambridge, 1992; and J. Katz, *From prejudice to destruction: anti-Semitism, 1700–1933*, Cambridge, Mass., 1980.

Specific national studies

D. Crew (ed.), *Nazism and German society*, London, 1994; S. Friedländer, *Nazi Germany and the Jews*, London, 1997; P. Webster, *Pétain's crime. The full story of French collaboration in the Holocaust*, London, 1990; P. Lendvai, *Anti-Semitism in eastern Europe*, London, 1971; and G. L. Mosse, *Germans and Jews. The right, the left and the search for a third force in Germany*, New York, 1970.

Hitler's anti-Semitism

I. Kershaw, *Hitler*, London, 1991, and *Hitler, 1889–1936. Hubris*, Harmondsworth, 1998; A. Bullock, *Hitler and Stalin. Parallel lives*, London, 1991; K. Cornish, *The Jew of Linz*, London, 1998; and J. Tolland, *Adolf Hitler*, New York, 1976.

Holocaust survivors and victims

P. Levi, *Moments of reprieve*, New York, 1985; B. Wilkomirski, *Fragments: A. Frank, the diary of a young girl*, New York, 1952; and E. Wiesel, *Night*, London, 1988.

Holocaust denial

D. Lipstadt, *Denying the Holocaust*, London, 1994.

Source collections

R. K. Chartock and J. Spencer (eds.), *Can it happen again? Chronicles of the Holocaust*, New York, 1995; and V. Klemperer, *I shall bear witness. The diaries of Victor Klemperer, 1933–41*, London, 1998.

Foreign reaction

B. Wasserstein, *Britain and the Jews of Europe*, London, 1979; J. Morley, *Vatican diplomacy and the Holocaust, 1939–43*, New York, 1980; W. Laqueur, *The terrible secret: an investigation into the suppression of information about 'Hitler's "Final Solution"'*, London, 1980; and M. Gilbert, *Auschwitz and the Allies*, New York, 1981.

Jewish resistance

Y. Bauer, *The Jewish emergence from powerlessness*, Toronto, 1979; and S. Krakowski, *The war of the doomed: Jewish armed resistance in Poland, 1942–44*, New York, 1984.

The historical debate

D. Goldhagen, *Hitler's willing executioners. Ordinary Germans and the Holocaust*, London, 1996; and M. Burleigh, *Ethics and extermination: reflections on Nazi genocide*, Cambridge, 1997.

Audio-visual sources

'Genocide', World at War series, Thames TV, 1973; 'The Nazis. A warning from history', BBC Video, 1998; and *Schindler's list*, Universal and Amblin Entertainment, 1993.

Chronology

1933 *30 January:* Adolf Hitler is appointed chancellor of Germany.

1 April: the Nazi Party initiates a one-day boycott of Jewish-owned businesses.

7 April: the Law for the Restoration of the Professional Standard of the Civil Service is enacted. Jews and anti-Nazi elements are dismissed from positions and functions in government and public institutions.

10 May: the public burning of books written by Jews and writers known for having anti-Nazi views is carried out. Such writers include Thomas and Heinrich Mann, Heinrich Heine and Albert Einstein.

14 July: a law is enacted which revokes the German citizenship that had been granted since 1918 to 'undesirable' persons (Jews from eastern Europe). This law does not target Jews, but because there was an increase in the number of Jews in Germany after the First World War Jews are the primary sufferers.

17 October: an order bans Jews from working in the German press.

1934 *1 April:* Heinrich Himmler is appointed head of the SS in Germany.

1935 *13 January:* the Saar region (which has been under League of Nations control since 1919) is annexed by Germany following a plebiscite.

16 March: despite its prohibition by the Treaty of Versailles, there is a renewal of conscription into the *Wehrmacht* (German army) in a law stating that only Germans of 'Aryan' descent may enlist in the *Wehrmacht*. Jews are dismissed from the German armed forces.

15 September: the proposed Nuremberg Laws are accepted during the Nazi Party's rally at Nuremberg. The two laws deal with protecting 'German blood and honour' and with preventing 'non-Aryans' from obtaining German citizenship.

14 November: the first ordinance of the Reichs Citizenship Law (a Nuremberg Law) is enacted. This defines the term 'Jew' according to racial principles and includes in its definition persons of Jewish descent, children and grandchildren of converted Jews and Jews of mixed lineage (*Mischlinge*).

1936 Jewish teachers are banned from teaching 'Aryan' children.

1937 *24 July:* the German Ministry of the Interior orders the separation of Jews from 'Aryan' guests at public baths and health resorts.

October: the 'Aryanisation' of Jewish businesses (the transfer of Jewish-owned businesses to 'Aryans') begins in Germany.

1938 *13 March:* the *Anschluss*, the annexation and integration of Austria into Germany, begins. All laws and restrictions which were instituted against the Jews of Germany are applied to the approximately 190,000 Jews of Austria.

26 April: it is decreed that Jewish property in Germany and Austria must be registered.

9 June: a Jewish synagogue is destroyed in Munich, Germany.

14 June: Jewish enterprises and businesses in Germany and Austria are formally classified as belonging to Jews.

July–September: Jewish doctors and lawyers in Germany are banned from practising among, or treating, non-Jews.

17 August: Jews in Germany are required to add to their names the middle name of 'Israel or 'Sarah' (depending on whether they are male or female).

October: a decree is issued ordering special identification cards for Jews in Germany. Passports held by Jews are marked with a large red 'J'.

26 October: 17,000 Jews with Polish citizenship living in Germany are expelled from the country and are deported across the border to Poland.

7 November: in Paris, Herschel Grynszpan, the 17-year-old son of a Jewish family expelled from Germany, assassinates Ernst vom Rath, a secretary to the German embassy in France.

9–10 November: Kristallnacht, a pogrom conducted throughout Germany, allegedly occurs as a punishment for the Jews for vom Rath's death. On that night 91 Jews are killed, 191 synagogues burnt down and 7,500 Jewish-owned shops looted; 30,000 Jews are sent to concentration camps.

12 November: the Jews of Germany are fined 1 billion Reichmarks as a penance for the murder of vom Rath. This must be paid to the German treasury.

15 November: Jewish children are banned from attending state schools.

November–December: decrees are issued restricting the movement of Jews within Germany and banning them from public places, entertainments and gatherings.

3 December: the compulsory 'Aryanisation' of firms and businesses owned by Jews in Germany is initiated.

8 December: the complete removal of Jews from teaching posts in German universities, institutions of higher education and research positions is ordered.

1939 *30 January:* on a day which commemorates the Nazis' rise to power in Germany (in 1933), Hitler, in his speech to the Reichstag, publicly proclaims the need for the annihilation of European Jews in the event of war.

15 March: German troops invade Czechoslovakia, ignoring the Munich Agreement (British Prime Minister Neville Chamberlain's peace pact with Hitler, signed in September 1938, which only allowed for Germany's annexation of the Sudetenland).

30 April: an official order regarding the tenancy of Jews is issued. It states that non-Jewish landlords may evict Jewish tenants.

6 July: initiated by US President Franklin D. Roosevelt, an international conference opens in Evian, France. The goal of the conference is to deal with the issue of the emigration of 'political refugees' (a euphemism for Jews from Germany and Austria). The conference, in which delegations from 32 countries take part, is a failure.

23 August: the Nazi-Soviet Pact (also known as the Ribbentrop-Molotov Non-aggression Pact) between Germany and the Soviet Union is signed. This agreement gives the Nazis a free hand to attack Poland.

1 September: Germany invades Poland, marking the beginning of the Second World War.

21 September: Reinhard Heydrich, Himmler's deputy, circulates a letter of instruction regarding the new Nazi policy towards the Jews. Heydrich defines the steps for the immediate future, which include the establishment of Jewish councils (*Judenrate*) and the creation of Jewish 'districts' in large communities. The 'ultimate aim' is presented in the letter/document as a goal which has to be kept absolutely secret; the 'aim' will be realised in later stages of development.

October: the first deportation of thousands of Jews from Bohemia-Moravia and Vienna (Austria) to the area of Nisko in south-western Poland begins. The area was planned and designated to be a Jewish 'reservation' in which the Jews are to be concentrated.

7 October: Himmler is appointed to the new position of Reich commissar for the strengthening of 'Germandom'. This position enables Himmler to deal with Jewish-resettlement plans and to interfere in the running of the German-occupied countries. Among his first steps is the expulsion of Poles and Jews from the western Polish territories that have been annexed by Germany.

26 October: in the newly established 'General Government' (the areas of Poland occupied by Germany in 1939 which were not annexed by the Third Reich) Jews are conscripted into forced-labour groups.

23 November: it is ordered that a yellow Star of David must be worn by all Jews living in the General Government area.

26 November: the governor general of Poland, Hans Frank, establishes Jewish councils in the General Government area.

November: the first Jewish ghetto, in Piotrkow Trybunal, Poland, is established.

1940 *9 April:* German troops invade Denmark and Norway.

27 April: Himmler orders the construction of a concentration camp at Auschwitz (Poland).

7 May: in Poland, the Lodz ghetto, the first major Jewish ghetto (containing 165,000 Jews), is closed off and isolated from the outside world.

10 May: Germany invades The Netherlands, Belgium and France.

22 June: France surrenders to Germany.

4 July: Berlin Jews are allowed to buy food only between 4 and 5 p.m.

July: a wave of persecution erupts against the Jews in Romania.

16 July: 7,500 Jews from the Saar, Baden (in Germany) and Alsace-Lorraine are expelled and deported to internment camps in France.

3 October: the *Statuits des Juifs*, anti-Jewish legislation limiting Jews' civil liberties, is enacted in Vichy, France.

16 October: the Warsaw ghetto is constructed in Poland; 400,000 Jews are closed in behind its walls.

1941 *January:* the expulsion of nearly 100,000 Jews from the environs of Warsaw to the Warsaw ghetto is carried out.

27 February: hundreds of Amsterdam Jews are deported to the concentration camp at Mauthausen (Austria), where they all perish within a short span of time.

6 April: German troops invade Greece and Yugoslavia.

April–May: simultaneously the 'Barbarossa Directive', announcing an operation to attack the Soviet Union, and the formation of the SS *Einsatzgruppen* are initiated. The *Einsatzgruppen* are special, mobile, killing units, whose task is to operate at the rear of the *Wehrmacht* and liquidate 'undesirable' elements, such as communists, political officers in the Red army and Jews. The *Wehrmacht*'s high command co-ordinates the operations of the *Einsatzgruppen* with the *Wehrmacht*, providing facilities for the special units.

22 June: the invasion of the Soviet Union and the implementation of Operation Barbarossa is started. Immediately following the invasion and capture of Soviet areas in the west the *Einsatzgruppen* begin the systematic mass murder of the Jews.

July: the mass murder of Jews from Vilna, Kovna and the Baltic states takes place (by the end of 1941 approximately 500,000 Jews will have been slaughtered by the *Einsatzgruppen*).

31 July: Göring issues the first written Nazi order about the 'Final Solution' (the total liquidation of the Jews) to the 'Jewish question' in Europe. The carrying out of the 'Final Solution' is delegated to Heydrich.

24 August: Hitler orders the official ending of 'Action T4', the 'Operation Euthanasia' in which 70,000 patients with hereditary illnesses have been killed (apparently the revelation of the action came as a result of the protests and pressure of church leaders).

28–29 September: 34,000 Jews are murdered at Babi-Yar, near Kiev, in the USSR.

September–October: the first experiments in killing prisoners in Auschwitz with Zyklon B gas take place.

10 October: the construction of the Theresienstadt ghetto in Czechoslovakia begins.

23 October: the emigration of Jews from the German Reich is forbidden. The migration of Jews from Poland and eastern European countries is banned from the spring of 1940.

October: the systematic deportation of Jews to the east begins. The camp at Birkenau is established as part of the network of the Auschwitz concentration camp. Birkenau later becomes the main extermination centre for European Jews.

December: Chelmno is established as the first killing centre for Jews in the Lodz area of Poland. This is the first extermination camp constructed under the plans for the 'Final Solution'.

1942 *January:* a Jewish fighting organisation (FPO) is established in the Vilna ghetto.

20 January: the Wannsee Conference, in which a plan to annihilate 11 million European Jews is presented to Nazi officials, takes place. The conference is a Nazi interdepartmental meeting chaired by Heydrich, which outlines and discusses the practical means for the execution of the 'Final Solution' of European Jewry. The plan includes statistics detailing the number of Jews in various countries (those under German control, as well as neutral and free countries).

1 March: the mass murder of Jews at Sobibor begins (about 250,000 Jews will be killed here. After the revolt of Jewish prisoners in October 1943 the Sobibor extermination camp is destroyed).

17 March: the mass murder of Jews begins at Belzec (approximately 600,000 Jews will be killed at Belzec before the destruction of the camp).

26 March: the deportation of Slovakian Jews, many of whom are young people, begins. Most are sent to Majdanek and Auschwitz.

30 March: the first transport of Jews from western Europe (France) arrives at Auschwitz.

May–June: the obligatory wearing of the Star of David, the mark of the Jews, is introduced in France, The Netherlands and Belgium.

22 June: the mass murder of Jews in Treblinka begins with the deportation of Jews from the Warsaw ghetto (about 300,000 Jews are deported from the Warsaw ghetto to Treblinka over six weeks. About 700,000 Jews from Poland and other European countries will ultimately be killed at Treblinka).

17 July: the first transport of Dutch Jews arrives at Auschwitz.

28 July: a Jewish fighting organisation (ZOB) is established in the Warsaw ghetto.

5 August: the first transport of Belgian Jews arrives at Auschwitz.

28 October: the first transport of Jews from Theresienstadt is sent to Auschwitz.

1943 *18–22 January:* the second deportation of Jews from the Warsaw ghetto occurs and instigates the first armed resistance and uprising of the Jewish fighting organisation in the ghetto.

2 February: the *Wehrmacht* surrenders to the Red army at Stalingrad, in the USSR.

15 March: the deportation of Greek Jews from Salonika to Auschwitz begins.

19 April: the liquidation of the Warsaw ghetto begins, as does the revolt of its inhabitants, which lasts until 15 May 1943.

April: the Bermuda Conference opens. Representatives of the USA and Britain discuss the issue of the potential rescue of Nazi victims and the problem of refugees. The conference closes without any practical agreements having been reached regarding the issue of Jewish refugees. The construction of the camp at Bergen-Belsen (Germany) for 'special categories' of Jews starts. The character and the task of Bergen-Belsen changes during the final stages of the war.

11 June: Himmler orders the liquidation of the ghettos in Poland.

2 August: Jewish prisoners in Treblinka revolt; the Nazis destroy this extermination centre.

16–23 August: the final deportation of Jews from Bialystok ghetto takes place and instigates a revolt.

3 September: a Jewish revolt occurs during the liquidation of the Lachwa ghetto (Poland) in western Byelorussia.

23 September: the Jews of the Tuchin ghetto (Poland), in the western Ukraine, resist and escape the Nazis.

September–October: the Danish underground rescues 7,500 Danish Jews, who, apart from a few hundred old and ill people, escape to neutral Sweden.

October: after the partial German occupation of Italy, about 8,500 Jews are captured and sent to Auschwitz.

1944 *March:* the *Wehrmacht* takes control in Hungary.

April: the extermination of Hungarian Jews begins (by the end of 1944 380,000 Hungarian Jews will have been sent to Auschwitz).

6 June: Allied troops land in Normandy, France.

24 July: Soviet troops enter Majdanek, the concentration and extermination camp.

7 October: Jewish prisoners in the *Sonderkommando* (special commando) revolt at Auschwitz.

27 November: Himmler orders the end of gassing at Auschwitz and the destruction of the gas chambers and crematoria at Birkenau.

1945 *18 January:* the evacuation of Auschwitz begins.

27 January: Soviet troops liberate about 7,500 Auschwitz prisoners, most of whom are either children or sickly.

January–April: the 'death marches' of the inmates of the concentration camps begin, with no defined destination.

5 April: US armed forces liberate Mauthausen.

15 April: British troops enter Bergen-Belsen.

29 April: US forces enter Dachau.

8 May: Germany surrenders unconditionally to the Allied forces; 6 million of the total number of 9 million European Jews have been killed by the Nazi regime.

November: the Nuremberg Trials of 24 leading Nazis begin and continue until October 1946. An international military tribunal sentences 11 Nazi leaders to death (Göring commits suicide before the sentence can be carried out).

1962 Adolf Eichmann is executed for war crimes following his trial in Israel in 1961.

Index

Index

Jewish–Bolshevik conspiracy, 15, 20
Jewish culture, in the ghettos, 55
Jewish population in Germany, categorisation of the, 26–7
Jewish resistance to the Holocaust, 2, 52–5
Jodl, Alfred, 84
Journal of Historical Review, 70, 71

Kapp, Wolfgang, 16
Karski, Jan, 62
Keitel, Wilhelm, 76, 84
Kershaw, Ian, 11, 36, 43
Klemperer, Victor, 29–30, 31
Krakowski, Shmuel, 2
Kristallnacht, 32–6, 44; Anglo-American attitudes to, 60–1

labour camps, 50, 57
Lammers, Hans, 22
Laval, Pierre, 77
Le Pen, Jean-Marie, 72
Liebknecht, Karl, 15
Lindberg, Charles, 59
Lipstadt, Deborah, 70
Lossow, General Otto von, 16, 17
Ludendorff, Erich von, 9, 16, 17
Lueger, Karl, 29
Luther, Martin, 5, 6, 7, 8, 13
Luxemburg, Rosa, 15

Madagascar Plan, 25–6, 37, 39, 44
Madole, James, 70
Marr, Wilhelm, 8
Marrus, Michael, 1, 2, 38–9, 39, 66
Marx, Karl, 7
Marxism, and anti-Semitism, 7, 8
Mein Kampf (Hitler), 10, 11, 17–18, 20, 32, 39
memories of the Holocaust, 91
Milch, General Erhard, 27
Mommsen, Hans, 1–2, 35, 40
moneylenders, Jews as, 5
Mosley, Sir Oswald, 59–60
Mussolini, Benito, 59–60, 78, 81

National Germanic League of Clerks, 8
Naumann, Bernd, 50
Nazi Party (NSDAP), 9, 12, 15, 18–19, 20, 59
Nazi persecution of the Jews, 22–31; in Austria, 28–9; emigration option, 22, 24–6, 36–8; foreign reaction to, 60–1; Jewish response to, 22–3, 29–30, 31; *Kristallnacht*, 32–6, 60–1; legal assault, 22, 23–4; and the Nuremberg Laws, 26–8, 30; one Jew's experience of, 29–30; shop boycott (1933), 23, 30
Nicholas II, Tsar of Russia, 5–6
Nuremberg Laws, 26–8, 30
Nuremberg War Trials, 83–4

Operation Barbarossa (German invasion of the USSR), 39, 40, 43–4
Operation Euthanasia, 39

Palestine: and death-camp survivors, 87, 88; Nazi resettlement of Jews in, 24–5, 37, 60, 65–6; *see also* Israel
Pan-German League, 8
Papen, Franz von, 19, 20
Pétain, Marshal Philippe, 61, 76, 77
Pius XI, Pope, 63, 78
Pius XII, Pope, 63–4, 78
Poland: death camps in, 41, 42, 47–8, 49; forced emigration of Jews to, 33, 37–8; German administration of, 80; post-war anti-Semitism in, 88, 91; Warsaw uprising (1943), 54–5, 57
Polanski, Roman, 54
Protestant churches: anti-Semitism and the Reformation, 5, 6, 7, 13; attitudes to Nazism, 64
'Protocols of the Elders of Zion', 16

Rabin, Yitzhak, 89, 90
Rassinier, Paul, 71
Rath, Ernst vom, 32–3, 36
Rathenau, Walter, 9, 15
Reformation, and anti-Semitism, 5, 6, 7, 13
Reitlinger, Gerald, 1
Riegner, Gerhart, 62
Rockwell, George Lincoln, 72
Romanian Jews, 79–80
Roosevelt, Franklin D., 37, 60–1, 65
Rosenberg, Alfred, 17, 28
Rousseau, Jean Jacques, 5
Ruhr occupation (1923), 16
Rumbold, Sir Horace, 59, 67
Russia: anti-Semitism, 5–6, 16; Bolshevik Revolution (1917) and German anti-Semitism, 9; *see also* Soviet Union

SA (*Sturmabteilung*), 23, 32, 33
Schacht, Hjalmar, 26
Schindler's list, 50
Schirach, Baldur von, 28
Schönerer, August von, 29
schools, in ghettos, 55
Second World War, and historical debate on the Holocaust, 39–41
Silverman, Sidney, 62
Slansky, Rudolf, 91
Slovak Jews, 79
Soviet Union: and Israel, 90; Nazi invasion of the, 39, 40, 43–4; *see also* Russia
SPD (Social Democratic Party), 7, 24
SS (*Einsatzgruppen*), 40, 44, 75, 82
Stalin, Josef, 65, 90
Stangl, Franz, 50
state-sponsored anti-Semitism, 5–6